Guide to Professional
Radio & TV Newscasting

FOR KIT
and
AMY and NANCY

No. 535
$9.95

Guide to Professional
Radio & TV Newscasting

by Robert C. Siller

TAB BOOKS

Blue Ridge Summit, Pa. 17214

57112

FIRST EDITION

FIRST PRINTING—MARCH 1972

Copyright © 1972 by TAB BOOKS

Printed in the United States
of America

International Standard Book No. 0-8306-2535-6

Library of Congress Card Number: 75-129043

Acknowledgments

Anyone who writes a book must face up, finally, to the impossible task of trying to thank everyone who contributed to it in one way or another.

In the beginning of this effort there was Verne Ray, Vice President of TAB BOOKS. He did three fine things: He conceived the project, selected the author, then left me alone to carry out the idea.

Going backward and forward from that point is much more difficult. For instance, how can I acknowledge the benevolent fate that opened the door for me to CBS News, an extraordinary organization that is devoted to responsibility and excellence in broadcast journalism? How can I pull from memory the names of so many creative people who taught me so much as we brushed against each other in the daily performance of our jobs?

Happily, I can thank Gordon Manning, Vice President and General Manager of CBS News, for the encouraging send-off he gave me in this endeavor and for his generous offer of whatever help I needed. My thanks go, also, to Emerson Stone, Director of CBS Radio News, for his kindness in helping me obtain certain material that I feel makes a substantial contribution to this book.

Only a few of the many broadcasters I have worked with actually are represented, but all the others hover somewhere in the background of whatever knowledge is set down here.

I must reserve a special place in these "credits," as I do in my heart, for so many of my associates of long standing on the CBS Morning News. There is the special delight for me of working so closely with Correspondent John Hart, whose high professional standards and integrity provide a model for anyone aspiring to a journalistic career.

In the day-in, day-out effort to put on a responsible and interesting television newscast, I've learned much about my craft—and life—from Phil Lewis, the Executive Producer of the CBS Morning News, Producer Dan Crossland, Ray Gandolf and so many others.

On those frequent occasions when I had specific technical questions, the experts who surround me at CBS News always were ready to help. Some who contributed so willingly are: video tape editor Morris Anton; radio news editor Marian Glick; associate director Herman Rich; film editor Albert Rausch; film laboratory technicians John Demeter and Dave Lundell; and Art Himmel of Q-TV, Inc.

Many helpful suggestions came from my long-time friend, the Rev. Herbert F. Lows, Director of Film Operations for the Broadcasting and Film Commission of the National Council of the Churches of Christ in the U.S.A.

Special thanks are due my young friends Norman Goldman, whose interest in this project is reflected in so many of the photographs, and Beverly Broadman, who helped get the most out of some difficult photographic problems. Jim Byrne, Manager of Publicity for CBS News, also was generous and gracious in providing illustrations.

There was a lot of help along the way, also, from Bill McKay, News Director for Television, WAKR, Akron, Ohio, and from Walter Hawver, then News Operations Manager of WTEN-TV in Albany, N.Y., who has since moved on to a new challenge.

R.C.S.

Contents

Illustration List

Preface

Although my background covers almost every phase of broadcast journalism except the broadcasting function itself, I did during my radio courses at Ohio University fancy myself as at least an occasional user of the microphone. But my first and lasting love is writing.

At one time, though, my career brought me in front of the microphone. In my first job out of college, as News Director of WELI in New Haven, Conn., there was that inevitable snowy day when the staff announcer didn't make it to work on time. An engineer literally pulled me from the news cubicle and, against my protests, put me on the air to broadcast a commercial. There wasn't time to look it over, much less time to do anything about it, and certainly no advance warning that I had to conclude the message by singing an awkward ditty, which I did...badly! Whatever minor demons of desire to broadcast that still lurked in my soul were exorcised that day. I have never since looked at a microphone without feeling at least some anxiety.

Then, too, during the course of my nine years with the American Broadcasting Company, there was one well-meaning friend who decided I should be a television reporter. When I brought back the film of my first interview and it revealed a perfectly composed subject and a terrified, camera-shy reporter, everyone agreed it was a simple lack of experience. When it happened the same way the second time, everyone agreed to my relief that my talent did not point in that direction.

I have had the good fortune to know and work with some of the finest broadcasters and newsmen in the business and remain content to let them or anyone but me do the air work. My admiration is limitless for those completely professional journalists who blend news judgment with fair play and use those attributes to communicate verbally and visually. I have also had the good fortune to share with some of these people the moments of high excitement over a job obviously well done. I have also shared with some of them moments of despair when the news was tragic in nature, and it fell to us to carry words of penetrating sorrow to the nation. I have joined some of these professionals in agonizing small and large points of contention in the desire to get the story and to get it right. Never in my lengthening years of experience, earlier with the American Broadcasting Company and more recently with CBS News, have I worked with anyone who used his position as newscaster for anything other than the purpose of trying to inform others truly and well.

The task I undertook here was assumed in just that same spirit, a desire to inform young men and women who are taking their first steps toward a career in the field that I never have regretted choosing for my life's work.

My assignment and purpose was to produce a "primer" on newscasting on radio and television. In a sense, then, this is a "how-to" book, and I have attempted to set down the basic information one needs to know to pursue a career before the microphone or camera. I hope the book is something more than just that, although I felt no need to get into some of the great, overriding philosophical questions of journalism as practiced by the broadcasting media. I do think, however, that my own deep feeling of commitment to the time-honored principles of journalism does show through the text.

This book was written during a time when there was a lot of talk about the role of the broadcast newsman in society. There has been much debate on the issue of journalistic advocacy. I do not hold with the notion that journalists must put aside the tradition of objectivity and consciously inject themselves personally into the news they cover and report, and thereby help lead the way to that great new world everyone talks about. The cornerstone of this advocacy argument is that there is no such thing as objectivity anyway, that journalists are human and unable to detach themselves from their own biases. Long years of experience have acquainted me with the difficulty of submerging my own feelings when it comes to handling news. Those years also have convinced me that dedication to that high goal of fairness is absolutely essential to the increasingly difficult task of reporting an increasingly complex society. Those who embrace the "journalism of advocacy" would push journalism into something it isn't and shouldn't be.

Rather, it seems to me, what is called for today is a "journalism of understanding," a craft practiced by well-educated, well-meaning people who are energized by the desire to inquire into and the privilege of publicly throwing light on the society in which they live. It is true that the adversary role that seems to pit journalism against government often is viewed in an unfavorable, even sinister light. Surely, there are those with pad and pencil, with microphone and camera, who do set out deliberately to destroy, but educated readers, listeners and viewers soon should detect the ax that is being ground. On the other hand, there are those in all walks of life who want and thrive on what Elizabeth Brew of the Atlantic Monthly has so aptly characterized as "the freedom of inattention." Those people must not be granted that sanctuary. It is the unending duty of responsible newsmen and women to look carefully and critically into what their government and their fellow citizens are doing, to report it as truly and fairly as they can, to expose where exposure is needed and to note also those activities that clearly are carried out in the public interest. This need for a "journalism of understanding" never will die unless freedom, itself, dies.

Robert C. Siller
Tappan, N.Y.

CHAPTER 1

The World of Broadcast Journalism

The pattern is familiar!

Breakfast time approaches. In homes across the United States, the housewife prepares the meal as the breadwinner shaves and dresses and the children head off to school. Thousands of families across the nation begin their day listening to radio and television sets spilling out information: the news of the world, the nation, and the immediate vicinity; weather forecasts, time checks, reports of traffic conditions, and all the other data that so many rely on.

At dusk, or after dinner, families gather in front of the television set to check once again on what kind of day it has been on earth, or out in space. And again just before bedtime millions find they must end the day as they began it, with a final review of the day's developments and a check on the weather outlook for the coming day. Thus, it is apparent that radio and television are an important part of the American way of life. Indeed, surveys show a continuing rise in the hours of television viewing, with families watching an average of about six hours each day.

Weekends bring only minor variations in familiar listening-viewing patterns, since portable radios provide news and entertainment on picnics, beach parties, autumn hikes; automobile radios keep a nation on the move constantly informed, and television sets serve as a "rallying point" while favorite newscasters detail the doings of each day.

The operative word, of course, is **favorite**. Radio and television newscasters, like stars of entertainment, sports heroes and other celebrities, attract a following. They must appeal to viewers if they are to remain on the air. Sometimes the reasons for popularity are all too frivolous—a resonant voice or an appealing way of parting the hair, for example. With an increasingly educated and sophisticated nation, however, the demands grow ever more substantial. Listeners and viewers are coming to expect, and rightly so, that highly-recognizable ring of authority behind the deep, rich voice. Moreover, they look beyond the face on the home screen for clear explanations. Newscasters on radio and television today must expect to encounter more critical and demanding audiences, a fact that imposes on those privileged to carry on in the tradition of the town crier the burden of presenting news with accuracy, perception and fairness. Personality, or "air presence," just is not enough anymore. Broadcast journalism has emerged from the era when the old "show biz" attitudes prevailed and has passed on to a mature, vital and responsible role in a news-conscious nation.

The growth and acceptance of broadcast journalism has been phenomenal. The first regularly-scheduled radio broadcasts were produced in 1920. As the decade of the 1970s began, there were more than 6,000 commercial AM and FM stations on the air, along with some 375 educational FM stations. Ninety-five out of every 100 homes in the United States had radios, with the average working out to about four sets per family.

Even faster has been the growth of television. The TV industry really dates back only to 1946, when six stations were on the air for the benefit of a few thousand people with receivers. At the start of the 70s, there were almost 700 Very High Frequency (VHF) and Ultra High Frequency (UHF) stations on the air, along with another 175 educational television stations. The number of receivers went over the 65,000,000 mark, with the percentage of color sets increasing quickly.

But even more remarkable than the physical growth of television has been the spectacular spread of its influence on viewers. Since 1959, the National Association of Broadcasters has commissioned a series of public opinion surveys. They show that, in spite of criticism from some politicians, the public is not only relying more on television for news but also is investing far more confidence in television news than in any other medium. A Roper Research Associates poll released by the NAB at the end of 1969 showed that TV had expanded its swiftly-won reputation as the most believable news medium to the point where it outranked newspapers by two-to-one in credibility. The actual poll figures showed that 44 percent of the respondents ranked television as the most believable news medium to 21 percent for newspapers. The survey also disclosed that 59 percent of those questioned rely on television as their primary source of news. Various studies reflect an almost constant upswing in viewer acceptance of television news. Both the Roper and R.H. Brusking & Associates organizations questioned people about where they usually went to get most of their news of the world. From a high of 51 percent in 1959, television's percentage went up to 60 percent by late 1970. An even sharper percentage increase was noted in the number of persons who would resolve conflicting or different reports on the same news story in favor of television over newspapers and magazines. The figures were 29 percent in 1959 and 50 percent in October of 1970.

Roy Danish, the Director of the NAB's Television Information Office, regards the 1970 figures as a "vote of confidence," which was particularly important "at a time when shocking and distasteful news events have generated criticism of traditional concepts of television journalism."

The NAB survey results have been reinforced by separate studies run by Sindlinger & Co., of Norwood, Pa., and by Louis Harris & Associates, Inc., of New York. The Sindlinger survey found that more adults in the United States now watch television during weekdays than read newspapers. The organization said its study, released in April of 1969, marked the first time since its series on media comparison began in 1959 that TV had overtaken newspapers in weekday exposure. The Harris survey was conducted for "Time" magazine and published in the issue of September 5, 1969. Nearly one-half of the 1,600 adult respondents across the country said they favored television if they could have "only one source of news." The Harris organization reported further that more than nine out of ten Americans said they watched TV news regularly, with the highest viewership among the middle-aged, middle-income individuals in medium-sized communities.

NEWS, COMMENTARY AND OPINION ON THE AIR

The highest challenge a broadcast journalist faces is his basic assignment. The newscaster on radio or television accepts the responsibility of keeping people informed to the best of his ability. He is the messenger of fact and a symbol of truth.

At the national level, on network radio and television, the newscaster presents information gathered and processed by regiments of highly-trained and experienced news personnel. At the local level, the resources and numbers of support troops are reduced sharply, but the function remains unchanged: to provide factual material in the most objective way.

This role of objectivity often is imperfectly understood by the audience, portions of which fail to differentiate between fact and opinion. Sometimes this merely is the result of excessive zeal, in which an individual who is wrapped up in a cause is blinded by his own enthusiasm. Thus, when the newscaster presents what he and his associates have constructed as an objective report on a controversial subject, the broadcaster often finds himself open not just to criticism but also to emotional abuse. Judgment, of course, is subjective and some people view information only through the narrow eye of their own experience and development, or a particular bias. So often one hears a listener or viewer complain that such and such a newscaster said that this or that is right, or that the newscaster has taken a stand on an issue or point of politics. If the newscaster is doing his job responsibly, he never does take a stand on any issue or even convey the notion that he favors one side against another. Scrupulous fairness is the hallmark of the newscaster. His task is to present the facts as best they can be ascertained, or to present as many sides as there are to any issue so that his listeners and viewers are better equipped to make up their own minds about what is right or wrong.

Confusion often arises in the minds of broadcast audiences when well-known correspondents verge into the area of commentary and analysis. Some networks and individual television stations permit thoroughly experienced reporters to go beyond the straight presentation of factual information. They are allowed to delve into some issue of the day in an effort to put the issue into some kind of perspective. Ordinary practice is to label that part of a newscast as commentary and analysis. Normally, the correspondent is forbidden to editorialize or express his own opinion on any controversy. Here, too, great privilege carries heavy responsibility. Any experienced writer knows all kinds of tricks through which he can build a case for his own point of view. Any correspondent who uses the air for his own purposes without regard for fairness risks losing the privilege. Most commentators are mature enough to give a balanced presentation, not just to protect their individual license but because they recognize it is the right thing to do.

Even with more air time devoted to news, television still provides only a small amount of time for commentary and analysis. It is interesting to note, in this light, that many of the best-known network television correspondents and newscasters also appear regularly on radio programs in which they step beyond the presentation of news and veer off into the area of commentary. Although, it is virtually impossible for a television newscaster to write all his own material, he usually writes whatever commentary he has time for. Thus, it seems that many TV newscasters have found a haven through which they are able to add a broader dimension to their coverage of the news.

Still another common practice in television is to designate one particular correspondent who delivers frequent or even nightly commentaries. This results in an obvious distinction between news and commentary.

The past decade witnessed another great stride toward responsibility in broadcasting with the increased exercise of the corporate right to editorialize on vital issues of the local community and the nation. However, whenever editorial opinion is broadcast, every precaution must be taken to make certain the listener or viewer knows that what he is hearing is not news but, rather, is opinion. The editorial position taken by a station should not be the view of any one individual; rather, it should reflect conclusions of an editorial board of station officials. Common practice is to have editorials read on the air by the station manager. Also, according to Federal Communications Commission Rules, any station that editorializes must give equal time for the presentation of opposing points of view.

NEWSCASTERS AND "NEWSCASTERS"

In the proper sense, a newscaster should be an educated, experienced radio or television journalist who devotes full time and energy to the task of disseminating information. Network newscasters who are heard and seen regularly ordinarily have the benefit of a lot of reporting and news writing experience. Those who occupy seats of influence and respect behind microphones and in front of cameras must demonstrate that maturity of judgment which makes them good newsmen first, with the ability to attract and even broaden their audience. Commercial broadcasting is a keenly competitive field at any level and the newscaster on radio or television must be good to stay on top.

On his journey up the career ladder, the broadcast journalist discovers his strengths and tries to perfect them. For those who reach the top, the selection of associates is vitally important. Network television production is so complex that many people are involved and the newscaster is thrust into a leadership role. When the planning and the production phases are completed, the newscaster pulls together the efforts of all those who work with him and he carries the finished product to the public. Because of this, he must try to surround himself with associates whose judgment he can trust and who are willing to feed his own strengths, surmount his weaknesses and thereby contribute to a better end product. Because of its less complicated production problems, radio news involves smaller teams than television to get the job done, but both media require smooth and harmonious teamwork.

At the local level, where budgets for news are thinner, a news broadcast often is the result of an individual effort, which makes sterner demands on the newscaster, himself. If he's responsible for the late night local radio news wrapup, the newscaster may well have spent a full, eight-hour day, or longer, writing and broadcasting other newscasts, and getting out and around the area to cover some events of the day. He may have lugged a tape recorder along to conduct interviews and then returned to his headquarters to edit the tape, write his script and, finally, to go on the air. His television counterpart may well have had a similar experience, perhaps even using a 16-millimeter camera to shoot silent film. The field of local television is home to many versatile newsmen who know how to use a camera, process film, edit a film to make a cohesive pictorial report, write a script and, ultimately, to go in front of the camera to broadcast the result of their own effort. This is hard, demanding work which, initially, is rewarded chiefly in personal satisfaction. The proper cultivation of those talents and techniques can carry the newsman to a place of prominence, locally, and financial security, or, if he wishes, on to bigger stations and better positions that pay handsomely.

The title of newscaster often is bestowed, if somewhat gratuitously, on individuals who perform a wide range of broadcasting functions, including reading newscasts. In the business, they are known as "announcer-readers." Since newscasting is not this person's sole duty or professional concern, it isn't fair to expect him to throw himself completely into the work, although he, too, must do more than just a creditable job to build his own professional standing.

Within the realm of the "part-time" newscaster is one type who rates mention in a negative sense. He has been dubbed the "ripper and reader." The term stems from the use of raw wire service material ripped off a teletype machine and read just to fill the time allotted to a newscast.

The Associated Press and United Press International provide "packaged" newscasts of national and international developments as part of the radio wire service. These summaries run the gamut from headline round-ups to full 15-minute newscasts which are formated so completely that they can be ripped from the printer and read. This sort of radio wire service is set up chiefly for the smaller stations that either cannot or choose not to employ trained news personnel and are content to entrust the news function to the "ripper and reader."

Mention of a rip-and-read newscaster recalls one of the classic tales to illustrate the last word in slipshod air work. It used to be that newswire packaged newscasts were so complete as to include a standard opening and closing, with blanks in the script for the reader to fill in his own name. As the story often is recounted, an individual ripped off one of these "canned" newscasts, sat down at the microphone without looking over the material and went on the air to declare:

"Now, the latest national and international news. Your reporter: (**ANNOUNCER'S NAME**)..." reading everything he saw in print. He overlooked the one addition the wire service just couldn't handle for him!

The key point to be emphasized about ripping and reading, however, is the sheer waste it makes of the station's own resources and the newscaster's own personality and individuality. Because of production requirements, it is almost impossible for the television newscaster just to rip and read. Thus, the practice is largely confined to radio stations and is indulged in sometimes by some surprisingly large and highly respected organizations. However, the fact cannot be ignored that there are two basic wire services to which most radio stations subscribe, or if not to both, then to one or the other. Therefore, since more than one station can be heard in most markets, it must soon become obvious to anyone who listens regularly that, as he switches from one station to another, he often hears not only the same news stories but also the same phraseology. While the practice of ripping and reading may save the station money, in the long run it can be costly in terms of public confidence. In an era in which the Federal Communications Commission is looking more and more critically into the public service performance of licensees, it might even contribute to eventual trouble at renewal time. It does take time and effort to rewrite wire service copy, but the job of keeping the audience informed suffers for lack of this individual effort.

THE CHANGING NEWSCAST

Broadcast journalism remains young and vibrant, as indicated by the periodic changes it has made. The hallmark of the radio newscast not many years ago was the 15-minute summary, a straight read-through by one man of a roundup of the top national, local, and international news of that day, complete with sports, a weather forecast, and a funny closing item. This kind of newscast does survive today, although its popularity has fallen off and its form, more often than not, now includes tape-recorded actualities of events or reports from correspondents or reporters in the field.

More recently, the 15-minute newscast has been replaced by shorter summaries presented more frequently. Many radio stations present at least a headline roundup and sometimes longer summaries on the hour and half hour. But the newest trend in radio news is the most complete possible reversal of the trend to short, newscasts: the "all-news" station which broadcasts nothing but news and news-related material.

These variations in radio news are matched by similar changes in television news. Network television news largely has passed beyond the era of the 15-minute summary and expanded to half-hour presentations, and in the waning months of the 1960s, even to the hour-long newscast as the great news-gathering organizations expanded their facilities, refined their techniques, and dug ever deeper into the enormous task of keeping the nation informed. Locally, expanding television newscasts often are meshed with the network productions, providing long and extensive coverage of the entire range of news.

In the end, of course, it is largely the "man out front," or newscaster, who bears the ultimate burden of broadcast journalism. He is heard and seen, believed and respected. He must sound well and look well. Above all, he must know what he is talking about.

NETWORK AND LOCAL NEWS

Several times we have referred to "network" and "local," or independent, radio and television. The average listener or viewer and the newcomer to broadcast journalism often has difficulty understanding the distinction between the two. It's doubtful that anyone who works for a network has not been approached by someone outside the field who opens the conversation with some remark such as: "Oh, you work for CBS News! That's Channel 2, isn't it? I watch your station all the time." The explanation is well meant, of course, but it conveys the usual ignorance of this basic division in broadcasting. Network and local operations, both in radio and television, employ wholly different approaches to news.

All individuals or groups of people wishing to go into either commercial or educational television broadcasting must apply for permission from the Federal Communications Commission to build a station. They might be interested in an amplitude modulation (AM) or a frequency modulation (FM) radio station or a UHF or VHF television station. Applications for licenses are subject to lengthy legal proceedings and, in the end, are granted partly on the promise that the new broadcaster will devote part of his air time to public service material, which includes news and news-oriented programming, especially local news. Licenses must be renewed every three years and the broadcaster must present evidence that he, has lived up to his public service commitment. Throughout the first 50 years of broadcasting, many radio and television stations performed all kinds of stunts in an effort to dodge their public service responsibilities and yet try to fake an attractive record for the renewal proceedings. Many broadcasters have managed to pocket a lot of extra profit in what they have saved on news and public affairs budgets. However, as the decade of the 70s began, there was strong evidence that many broadcasters who have dealt lightly, or not at all, with their public service responsibilities are in for trouble. Indeed, more and more groups of citizens and persons with special interests are challenging the licenses of stations with an eye to forcing much more responsible activity in the public service sphere, or even getting that broadcasting franchise for themselves on the promise they will do more to serve the public.

Primarily, the individual or group operating anything from a 250 to a 50,000-watt AM station, an FM station or a TV station is expected to provide listeners and viewers with its own coverage of news of the city or town in which the station operates and the listening or viewing area it covers. The public service commitment usually is considered to include such additional programming as local news documentaries, local election campaign discussions, debates and coverage, religious programs and whatever else the station management decides it can broadcast in the public interest. Indeed, at this stage in the development of broadcasting, there is increasing use of both radio and television to stimulate an informed citizenry by providing live coverage of town meetings, city council meetings and those discussions so vital to the proper functioning of local government.

As the name denotes, an independent radio or television station is programmed individually by its management. The only national programming they carry ordinarily would be entertainment shows bought through a syndication arrangement. In the news and public affairs area, the independents are on their own. Their competition at the local level is the network affiliate, a station of whatever size and power whose owners have determined they want to broadcast a combination of local and national programming. The management thus elects to affiliate with a regional or national network. What this means, basically, is that instead of developing or controlling everything it puts on the air, the affiliate station sets aside a certain amount of time each day to carry the programs produced by the network and fed to all its outlets all over the country. The affiliates get newscasts that encompass the broad sweep of national and international news, as well as documentaries, public service programming and entertainment matter. The affiliates bring in extra audience that enables the network to charge higher national advertising fees, in which the affiliates share.

The major radio and television networks are the American Broadcasting Company, the Columbia Broadcasting System and the National Broadcasting Company. There are about 50 regional networks and groups of radio and television stations. The FCC does not license the networks, although FCC Rules limit the networks to seven owned and operated (O & O) AM stations, seven FM stations and seven television stations, of which not more than five TV stations can be in the Very High Frequency range. There is no limit on the number of affiliates and, indeed, there is keen competition to get the best stations in important markets to sign up with a network. The ABC radio network, for instance, claims some 900 affiliates, while its TV network lists some 150 primary affiliates. The NBC radio network has some 220 stations, with the television network made up of about 200 affiliates. The CBS radio network numbers almost 250 stations, and the CBS television network includes some 200 stations.

In radio and in television, these vast networks are supplied by telephone lines. The major networks are headquartered in New York City, where the news division of each produces heavy schedules of daily newscasts and documentaries. While they sometimes use their facilities interchangeably, the networks news department ordinarily is separated from those of the affiliate "flagship" station in New York City. The so-called New York "flagship" stations are WABC and WABC-TV, WCBS and WCBS-TV and WNBC and WNBC-TV. The network news departments do not service any one station but rather all the owned-and-operated stations and as many affiliates as choose to carry the productions.

CHAPTER 2

Basic "Equipment"

In order to inform others, one must be informed.

For the broadcast journalist, then, the bedrock of a career has to be a broad and solid education. There is no need to dwell here on the general benefits of a good education or the precise form of schooling that someone aiming toward broadcast journalism should pursue. Many schools of journalism determined long ago that a rich blend of liberal arts and "technique" courses is ideal. There is no denying the philosophy, and little to deter the serious student from achieving just that.

Broadcast journalism has moved into its own age of specialization, but at a crawl. Thus, the radio or television newscaster comes to grips daily with more interesting and more complicated subjects than ordinary mortals can possibly master. Newspapers and wire services are highly departmentalized, with their own or syndicated specialists writing on politics, international affairs, economics, the arts, entertainment, sports, and even on radio and television! Only the major broadcasting networks and the wealthiest independent radio and television stations can (or do) afford the luxury of expertise and hire knowledgeable persons to single out and report on significant developments within their area of special interest. Even the general newspaper reporter ordinarily is called upon to deal only with one story in the course of a day's work. The only newspaper functions that correspond in any degree to the demands made upon the newscaster are those performed by members of the rewrite staff, which may handle a series of different ideas each day, or the editors who ride herd daily on the reams of copy on a wide variety of subjects.

For contrast, listen to any radio or television newscast, anytime. Whether the broadcaster has written his own copy or not, he might well be called upon to deal in any one production with anything from a war story to a local murder or to a seemingly inexplicable, sudden drop in the price of gold on the international markets. Then, just to round things out, he may have to touch on a sports item. He is expected to sound knowledgeable on everything he reads.

There is no denying that the broadcast newsman of the past had one thing going for him as a buffer against mental strain: so little time was devoted to any story that the newscaster rarely had to extend himself to explain anything in detail or to take any great pains to point out its relevance. That job was left to the documentarians. Radio and television news skimmed the surface of a story and left it to the newspapers and news magazines to fill in the important background and to explore the minutiae that so often tell so much more about a story or give it life. As radio and television news time expanded, however, broadcast journalism has been able to improve and strengthen the flow of the information it provides.

EXPERIENCE

Experience is the partner of education in the professional pursuit of any career. Young people with fine academic records often find themselves caught in the dilemma of failing to qualify for the positions they seek because they weren't able to pile up experience while getting an education. The practical way to break that unhappy cycle is to put in at least a brief apprenticeship at a small station and collect some experience.

Experience, like education, should be measured in terms of quality rather than quantity, but the whole question of career development is so entirely personal and individual that one really must feel his own way. An alert awareness of one's own needs and capabilities is the only true guidance system to carry a person through the uncharted seas of a career. One learns about himself as well as his work as time goes by. The chances are that if an individual convinces himself he can no longer learn from the job he has, it is time for him to move on.

Before making any more, though, you should have some idea of where you wish to go in your chosen field. With some sort of goal in mind, the individual regularly must review his own accomplishments and try to fit them into the constantly changing needs of his profession. This isn't exactly easy. It may be comforting to remember, however, that every other career seeker has the same problem!

VOICE AND APPEARANCE

There was a time in radio when the sole criterion for employment was a characteristic described as a deep and

26

mellifluous voice. This practice was prevalent in newscasting as well as every other branch of the business. Radio, in effect, was in love with its voice, and the sound that emanated from the home set often was considered much more important than what the voice said.

Time was in television, too, when good looks were much more important than anything else in the selection of an individual to appear on camera. A set of finely matched, white teeth and a pleasing personality counted for more than intelligence, even among some who were chosen to inform others.

Fortunately, this day has passed in the news areas of both media. As the moguls of Hollywood came to realize, there is a difference between the make-believe and real worlds, and that in the very real world of news, information, and communications of ideas, substance is everything and appearance is minor in importance.

Long ago, the late Elmer Davis rasped into a microphone every weeknight, and at other intervals, and helped to prove the point that the newsman with something important to say could successfully combat the inane theory that the voice beautiful was essential for radio. As he did in many areas of human endeavor, Davis lighted the way for others with courage and conviction.

It would be ridiculous to deny, of course, that the competent journalist who just happens to be handsome and blessed with a deep, resonant voice has a lot going for him. In the end, however, he still must capitalize on his substance as a communicator, and in a day of deepening maturity in broadcast journalism, the individual with lesser physical attributes should not be put off.

THE QUESTION OF STYLE

The ability to communicate, via microphone or camera, is the essence of broadcast journalism. This ability has its origins in thought processes and carries over into the area of self-expression. It is a highly individualized or personal ability, partly innate and partly acquired.

Because of its very public nature, broadcasting provides its own school for those who would take the time to attend. As the aspiring broadcast journalist pursues his formal education, at the high school or college level, he can also begin to develop a style of his own. He can do this by studying the styles of others already operating in his chosen arena. All it takes is a radio and television set and the willingness to spend time in study and analysis of the work that is performed on both. Radio provides more of a range of styles, especially in rural areas of the United States where more radio stations than television outlets are available to the audience.

For the novice, then, the first step toward a career in broadcast journalism should be a survey of current work. Listen carefully to as many different newscasts and newscasters as you can find on your radio. After a broad survey of everything available, narrow the field by listening again, several times, to the newscasters who appeal to you. Then, try to discover for yourself what it is that did appeal to you. What was it that sets that particular newscaster apart in your judgment? The serious student soon will discover that he is pulling the newscast apart on two levels: first, he considers the range of information that is conveyed, and second, he thinks about the manner in which it is presented. At this beginning stage of this "home study" program, perhaps it will be more productive to concentrate on the subjective consideration of style. Value judgments on news, per se, really come later.

Because of the stratification of broadcasting, it is likely that the novice will find the newscasting styles that appeal most to him among the ranks of the network broadcasters. These are the men and women at the top. Taken as a whole, they represent just about everything there is to show in the range of style, from the highly dramatic delivery that often tends to sensationalize the news to the cool, calm, down-played manner or intellectual approach. Somewhere within those extremes, the student can stake out his own initial claim. He will want to move around later, but it is a starting place in that lifelong drive to fine one's self, one's own style, one's own place in a chosen field.

Obviously, this same "home study" technique can be carried over into television, and must be for anyone seriously thinking of trying to make his way in the medium. It's right there for the taking. All it costs is some effort.

The point to be made here simply is that anyone aspiring to a career in broadcast journalism must find the way in which he is most effective in expressing himself, or communicating. Clarifying your ability to express yourself cannot possibly do any harm, regardless of the career you ultimately pursue. Learning from others is essential.

PRACTICE, PRACTICE, PRACTICE

The "home study" approach to radio and television-news easily can be expanded into an "off-the-job" routine of practice and development. It would seem obvious that someone with the desire to communicate verbally must make an early commitment to refine his own speech. There is, of course, a difference between "on-the-air" diction and personal conversation, but it can only help the aspiring newscaster to practice the beneficial technique of speaking clearly at all times.

For the student, opportunities for preliminary exposure to the microphone often can be found in radio clubs in high school, and the often elaborate radio and television stations operated by colleges and universities. Each instance is another world of elementary experience that is available for the taking.

Even the isolated individual need not despair of trying out his abilities. Anyone can put together his own version of a newscast from newspaper clippings, then sit down before a makeshift microphone or mirror to practice reading it. Tape recorders today can be bought with limited funds, and the novice can spend productive hours taping his own words. On playback the beginner has an opportunity to analyze his work and to work on his weaknesses and strengths.

For the avid young person, there will be learning opportunities offered by the nearest radio and television stations. Someone with a desire to learn about broadcasting seldom will be turned away if he goes about the search considerately. Newsmen and women generally are extroverts. Usually, they are approachable and, when time permits, like to talk about their work. The expenditures of some time at a radio or television station, offering to lend a hand with some of the menial chores, often will result in some special attention and a boost along the way. There will be times when the hectic pace of a hectic business will rule out any assistance at the moment and might even result in the seeker getting snapped at, but properly timed advances and a courteous approach often will win rewards.

STRONG NERVES

It would be wrong not to mention one other physical characteristic that the business demands of the broadcast newsman: an ability to remain calm under trying circumstances. The newscaster or anyone who wants to broadcast must have at least a trace of the "ham" in his or her basic makeup. Either he must start with the ability to perform in public or be able to develop that ability. "Mike fright" and "camera consternation" are real dangers that must be recognized and overcome. Here again is a problem that defies any general remedy. The individual with sufficient desire to do the job will learn how to handle his problem in his own way.

Similarly, it should be recognized even before an individual commits himself to the field that broadcast journalism often is a business of high tension for everyone involved in the production or delivery of a newscast. If it can get rough for the support troops, think what it is like for the person behind the microphone or in front of the camera. Broadcast journalism is an up-to-the-minute business. This often means that last second changes must be made in productions or even while the production is on the air. The newscaster must be flexible enough to adjust to often radical changes dictated by a breaking or changing news story. He must have the ability to conceal from the audience the turmoil that often exists as the production develops. He simply cannot become rattled by anything that normally would unnerve anyone. In a sense, this is a throwback to the old "show biz" attitude that the "show must go on," but it is more than just that. A newscaster doesn't just walk away from the microphone or camera in the middle of a production even though he might feel like doing just that. The time must be filled, the assignment must be carried out, and if the individual's mental attitude is such that he breaks down or blows up under pressure, he better look for another line of work!

SOME "TOOLS" OF THE TRADE

Not so long ago the actual "tools" of the newscasting trade were few. The broadcast journalist of radio's peak years carried most of his equipment in his head. Beyond his brain, he needed an up-to-date dictionary to find the right words and how to pronounce them, a trustworthy typewriter, and an accurate stopwatch for timing his script and to keep handy while broadcasting. Those tools still are essential. Today, however, the radio newscaster must be familiar with the workings of a tape recorder. His television counterpart must assimilate a wealth of technical information about film and video tape, as well as learn to operate various cameras, as we discuss later.

CHAPTER 3

Preparing for the Newscast

The radio or television newscast is a structured affair. For real and practical reasons, nobody ad-libs either one. Only the most gifted conversationalist, and one with a photographic mind, could sit down in front of a microphone and rattle off the latest news of the world and do so in a logical pattern and within a tight framework in time. With its often complex production problems, this "winging" of a television newscast is utterly unthinkable. Thus, the broadcast journalist expresses himself first in the planning of his newscast, then in the scripting of the production, and, ultimately, in the actual broadcasting of it.

At the local level, the newscaster generally is expected to take an active role in preparing his radio or television production. In radio, more often than not, this is simply a one-man job. Only the most devoted of the independent radio stations employ one or more writers for the specific purpose of writing news for broadcast.

At the network level, the trend in recent years has veered increasingly toward the practice of employing only seasoned newsmen who can write their own copy. In bygone years the major radio networks hired extensive staffs of writers just for the task of writing newscasts; more and more, now, writers serve as "operations" men who monitor incoming reports from correspondents and reporters around the world for factual accuracy and timeliness. "Operations" men also time and edit taped audio reports filed by reporters. In some network newsrooms, writers rarely or perhaps never actually do write a newscast. That function is assumed by the broadcaster. The practice has merit in that there is no time lost in allowing the newscaster to familiarize himself with someone else's copy and since he has written it himself, he certainly should be able to read it!

In television news, also, the performer at the local level is expected to contribute heavily to every preliminary stage as well as the performance. Network television, with its unique production problems and last-minute changes, relies on extensive production teams to carry a newscast through from inception to execution. At both levels, however, the

57112

newscaster himself ordinarily sets the tone of his own role in his production. It boils down to a question of personality. There are those more energetic individuals who simply must have a hand in everything as well as those who will sit back and let others do as much as they will. It stands to reason that personal involvement has to add to the end product. When crises do arise on the air, as they do from time to time, it is the radio or television newscaster most familiar with the overall production who will be better able to ride with or cover the unexpected situation and get out of it gracefully, while his less interested colleague is more likely to wind up with "egg on his face!"

"READING-IN"

Normally, newsroom procedure permits the newscaster to begin his work day by "reading-in," which, as the phrase implies, means gathering his source material and familiarizing himself with it. Available time determines how much reading-in there is and it is to be assumed there just never can be enough time to digest all the data coming from so many different directions. Even the smallest radio stations must subscribe to a wire service as the basic source of information. The more news-oriented small radio and television stations use both the Associated Press and United Press International services. Their constantly chattering printers double the supply of information and the time needed to cull the reams of paper for the pertinent. The television newscaster must also familiarize himself with the pictorial material available to him in still photographs, film or video tape. In network news, the river of source material rarely falls below flood level. To the voluminous AP and UPI reports often is added the output of the British news service, Reuter. Whether newscasters are dealing with local or national and international news, they should check the best newspapers available to see how the print media is treating the major stories. With the torrent of information to be sifted and sorted, the most logical approach in television is the "team" effort. The newscaster at any level, however, must devise his own system for digesting the source matter.

At most levels of radio, ordinarily the newscaster selects the items he wishes to include in a given newscast, applying his experience and skill as a broadcast journalist to choose the significant and relate it in an interesting way. He must determine how much time each item merits, its proper placement within the newscast, and the approach he wants to take. These decisions are subjective to a degree and, taken as a whole, make up what is known as news judgment. Because radio reuses the top stories again and again, the newscaster always must look for some legitimate way to update individual items, or move them along in time. This requires a close survey of the wire service reports and frequent rewrites of breaking stories. This is radio's stock in trade. Radio has the capability of informing instantly. When a "bulletin," or news story of overriding importance, is put out by the wire services or, in the case of the networks by its own news-gathering organization, radio can broadcast that information almost instantaneously. That is the extraordinary, however, and the radio newscaster's day-to-day concern is to give the important local, national or international news.

The local newscaster might also be expected to conduct telephone or tape recorded interviews for inclusion in his newscasts. The daily work load can vary tremendously, from two or three to half-a-dozen broadcasts, depending on length and the total time the station management is willing to devote each day to news. Whether the actual work load is light or heavy, the newscaster on radio generally can expect to put in a busy day of reading, writing and broadcasting. The more industry and integrity he brings to his job, the busier he will be, of course, but also the more satisfied and rewarded, too.

USING THE WIRE SERVICES PROPERLY

Basic to the preparation of any newscast, whether radio or television, is a working knowledge of the way the major wire services operate. For most stations, the Associated Press and United Press International provide most of the information that is broadcast. Recently, the British news service, Reuter, has expanded its coverage of the United States and, with its traditionally strong coverage of the Middle East and Europe, provides a helpful adjunct to the domestic services for those network news operations and stations with well-rounded news operations. Even the networks that employ so many reporters, writers and editors lean heavily on the wire services both as the point of origin of news coverage of a particular story and for the details of events that do not merit audio or visual coverage.

The amount of information put out by the wire services is staggering. Twenty-four hours a day, seven days each week, the wire services' printers clatter away, spilling out stories on every kind of development anywhere that human contact can be made. If wire service reporters cannot get to the place

Bank of wire service printers in soundproof enclosures in the central newsroom at the CBS News headquarters in New York. (Courtesy Norman Goldman)

where news is happening, the service might have a "stringer," or part-time reporter who knows that particular area, cover the event or else telephone someone who can provide reliable information about what happened. From a telephone or telegraph office nearest the scene, the wire service reporter forwards his account to the nearest regional wire service bureau, which in most instances is located in the state capital. If the reporter is a bona fide newsmen or a staff member, the bureau manager or editor probably will just relay his report to a regional headquarters where it can be fed to the entire wire service network of thousands of radio and television stations and newspapers. The major wire services, like the broadcasting networks, maintain headquarters and central filing operations in most major cities.

Because of the volume of information they generate every day, the wire services have had to separate their output into several different wires. Basic national service is provided in the so-called "A" wire which is prepared primarily for newspapers. It is written in newspaper rather than broadcast style. The "A" wire of both AP and UPI carries all information that the editors designate as news of importance and interest to people in every part of the country. Reinforcing the "A" wire output with news of narrower or specialized interest are a separate sports wire and the "B" wire which normally are found only in the most affluent and news-oriented stations or in network news headquarters. In addition, the wire services offer state wires for their clients as well as separate radio wires.

In theory, the radio wires are a special service tailored to the needs of broadcasters by rewriting the "A" wire stories in what is supposed to be broadcast style. In practice, the wire services often use their radio wires as a training operation, putting their newest writers to work beating out all kinds of quasi-newscasts. By most standards, these radio wire round-ups still require close and often heavy editing at the very least and more often than not they need extensive rewriting. There is at least a sampling of regional, state and local news serviced to radio wire clients, but any station with more than a minimal concern for local news would have to build substantially on the radio wire coverage to do justice to the community it serves. For additional fees, the wire services offer special local coverage of the major metropolitan areas.

The AP is a newspaper cooperative and it requires member-clients to file copies of their news stories with the service to be incorporated as desired in AP's daily file. When a newspaper has developed an exceptional story for which it wants to retain exclusive use or credit, it must have that story copyrighted. Often, when a newspaper has generated an important story from its own sources and does not wish to name those sources, the wire services will pick up the story but will "hang it on" the newspaper by attributing it directly to the newspaper.

Because the two major wire services are newspaper-oriented, their daily file is set up for the convenience of newspaper editors. Both the AP and UPI divide their "A" wire coverage into two 12-hour periods, design as the AM and PM cycles that correspond to the needs of morning and afternoon newspapers. Sometimes between midnight and 1 AM, for instance, the two services begin each new day by sending out their PM budget. This is a listing and brief description of the major news stories the services plan to file within the next few hours, or in ample time for the newspapers of that afternoon. The budget will give an indication of how many words it will file on each story to give newspaper makeup editors some ideas of how much space they should reserve for those stories they plan to use. The budgets also contain some indication of whether or not any story can be expected to change materially before publication time; in such instances the wire services will file new leads. The wire service budget stories are set up in such a way that they can "stand up" for later newspaper editions simply by substituting the new lead for one or more paragraphs. When a first, second, third or whatever number of new leads are filed, they carry pickup lines indicating where the prior stories should be joined to that new lead. The trick for the newspaper wire editors or broadcast writer or newscaster is to make absolutely certain he has kept complete track of changes in each news item so that his source copy always is right up to the minute. Similarly, it is common for errors of fact and just plain "typos," or typographical errors, to get out on the wires. The alert editor is expected to catch most of those errors on his own, but all who use wire service copy must remain alert at all times for those corrections that come along well after the original error and often make substantive changes in the story. For the broadcaster with one or more daily deadlines, this means that the wire service printers must be checked every few minutes and the copy cleared and brought up to date frequently to stay ahead of that constant flow of information.

Beyond the budget stories, of course, are those "breaking" news stories that come along every day and which hardly can be anticipated. A story of the first magnitude, or great interest to great numbers of people, wins the wire service designation of bulletin. Reuter has its own, typically British designation for a bulletin. It calls a bulletin a "snap." However named, bulletins are signaled by the ringing of five bells on the wire service printer. Normally, bulletin matter is moved in "takes," which is to say that a first paragraph is cleared as quickly as possible to get the broadcasters and newspaper editors moving on a major story. This is the area in which broadcast journalism is so effective in that it can get the word out to its listening-viewing area immediately, largely because newspaper editors know they can't possibly compete in the speed of news transmission, the old practice of putting out extra editions for major news has been abandoned. Often, a radio or television station is able to put its bulletin on the air on the basis of just that first paragraph. Indeed, in the case of the death of a prominent figure, the broadcast bulletin might be only one sentence or so, just enough to identify the person, announce the death and perhaps give his age or some detail. Frequently, this information is respected for clarity and the bulletin is signed off with the advice to the listener or viewer to stay tuned for further details on regularly scheduled newscasts. In other cases, where the bulletin story is breaking over an extended period of time, broadcasters usually will keep interrupting regular programming to keep their audience informed of developments. In very occasional circumstances, the story might be so important that regular programming is suspended and the radio or television station marshals all its resources to cover it in infinite detail.

When a story breaks of more than normal consequence but not the importance of a bulletin, the wire services editors often put the word "urgent" on it to alert news editors of a story to which they feel has special significance. This, of course, gets one into the subjective areas of news judgment. News editors are human. It is not uncommon for them to overreact or, at first blush, to misjudge the importance of one story or another. Still another possibility exists in that the correspondent at the scene makes a similar mistake in judgment and panics the wire editor into putting out a bulletin unjustifiably. When cooler judgment takes over, the only thing the wire service can do is to issue a kill on the bulletin, as it would on an erroneous story that had been dispatched under the same circumstances. In the case of bulletin matter, it is the radio or television station that is more likely to get stung, again because of the speed with which it can get the story on the air. Thus, this complex question of news judgment evolves along the chain of news dissemination to the editor at the radio or television station. He can take one wire service at face value if, indeed, it moves a bulletin ahead of the others, or else he can play it safe and wait until that information is more or less confirmed by appearing on another service. In most cases, the major services will be only minutes apart in moving bulletin matter, but those minutes can be precious in the furious competition among individual stations and especially in network news operations. Often it is this very spirit of competition that causes false information to be put out. This is an always difficult situation; a newscaster or an editor who makes a decision to go ahead can suffer at least embarrassment and possible reprimand if something goes wrong with the information. On the other hand, he can get in just as much trouble if he fails to put it on the air and it turns out to be right.

Unfortunately, in spite of all kinds of precautions and often even diligent efforts to get at the facts, much erroneous information does creep out on the wires, into newspapers and onto the air. It is the bane of every newsman's existence that the wire services so often can be so far apart on the details of the same story. Frequently, it is difficult to believe the services are covering the same story. Anyone with any experience in using wire copy can cite instance after instance in which AP said one thing, UPI something else and, not infrequently, Reuter had still another version. Quite another kind of problem arises when, for instance, a network correspondent or reporter is at the scene of a news happening and the information he relays doesn't square in every detail with what one or more of the wire services says. The accepted rule of thumb is that you believe your own man. If he is wrong consistently, he won't be your man very long.

When you have no one at the event, such discrepancies can be much more difficult to resolve. The most practical method is to check them out for yourself, if time and the news department budget permit. A telephone call might be all that it takes to get an authoritative version of what actually happened. Of course, if your organization subscribes to the three major services and two of the three agree, the normal thing is to go with the consensus. Usually, a newsman over the years develops a preference for one of the wire services. If he can't check the story or find agreement about the disputed detail somewhere, he is faced ultimately with the need to go with the service of his choice. All too often, of course, radio and television stations subscribe only to one service, and thus never do realize how much misinformation they put on the air. It should be noted, however, that this information ordinarily involves some detail of a story, not its essence. Mostly, the disagreement can be found in such things as the number of people involved in an event which can be important to a particular story. In that case, a value judgment must be made. If, on the other hand, it is clear the disputed figure or fact is not essential to the story, the obvious move is to omit that element. In extreme cases of conflicting information, the newscaster sometimes is driven to the device of "hanging it on" the wire services, by saying that AP says this and UPI says that. This kind of approach is to be employed only when the detail in dispute is absolutely essential.

TEAMWORK AND TELEVISION NEWS

Largely because of production problems, a television newscast even at the local level must involve the work of more than one man. The newscaster performs the same chores of judgment as to the news content of his production as does his radio counterpart; in addition, of course, he works in the pictorial elements.

No matter how large or small the television news production team is, adequate communication among its members is absolutely essential. In a basic one-camera, small-station operation, the newscaster and director must get together before the broadcast to check over the script and make absolutely certain that each knows what is going to happen. Multiply this need by five or perhaps as many as ten times when it comes to a major network newscast. Teams of writers, editors, film editors, graphic artists, associate directors, directors, associate producers, and producers must coordinate their functions with the newscaster and, in all likelihood, with an executive producer who is in overall charge of the broad and diversified production. The effort to communicate with millions of viewers can easily be frustrated by the lack of communication among members of the television news team. If the director in the control room is not sure which way the newscaster intends to turn, for example, the result can be that embarrassing moment when the newscaster peers into a camera that isn't on him. If a still photograph has been chosen to illustrate a particular point without the newscaster's knowledge, he can look silly. There are hundreds of ways in which the man in front of the camera can be made to look ridiculous, and just as many reasons why he should not be.

The primary way of bringing everyone together with the same purpose and instructions is the television script. It conveys not only the news, itself, but also the audio and visual cues required to carry the production through to a successful conclusion.

CHAPTER 4

Writing for Broadcast

The aspiring broadcast journalist must learn to write as well as to read clearly and well, since the trend in broadcasting now is to employ only those newsmen who can adequately perform the dual function of reading their own copy on the air. Actually, anyone in any field of endeavor should want to develop the facility to express himself in a crisp, clear, concise way, and there is no surer way to crystallize one's thoughts then to commit them to paper. The radio and television newscaster does, of course, have more than the ordinary problem of self-expression when he sits down to write. There are vast differences between writing and speaking styles and he must first find then cultivate that method of putting down on paper the words that convey his own thoughts in a way that he can read with comfort and certainty. The newscaster must determine his own reading speed so that he can write to the tightest of time limitations under any kind of pressure.

Here, again, is an area in which the young aspirant doesn't have to wait for formal training to begin to feel his way toward a style. The interested young person can find constructive pleasure by taking his home study of newscasters' styles another step along the way by trying to write his own newscasts. With an idea fixed in mind of how an admired professional delivers his newscast, the beginner can take a copy of a local newspaper, select any number of stories that interest him and write them the way he thinks he would handle them in an actual broadcast. Then, with copy either written by hand or typed, the aspirant can sit or stand in front of a makeshift microphone or a mirror and practice delivering his own newscasts. Professionals constantly refine their style by day-to-day practice and experience, and in the same manner the would-be broadcast journalist can give himself a valuable head start. For the serious student, again, it should not take long to begin to learn what kind of individual effort is required to do the job. Obviously, this same goal can be achieved by practice in high school and college radio and television facilities.

The essential point here is that a skill in writing for broadcast is not truly a creative talent but more of an acquired facility that can be sharpened and improved constantly, and it develops best with daily practice. This is not to imply that news writing cannot be approached in a creative or imaginative way. There will always be room for the individual with some unique, new way to say things, if indeed his uniqueness and newness contribute to understanding. It cannot be overemphasized, however, that the basic stuff of news is fact, or what is taken at the time to be fact, and it cannot be subject to creative adaptation, embellishment or change. The manner of the presentation leaves room for imagination, but not the material itself.

ONE CHANCE ONLY

The broadcast journalist must approach the writing task with a keen awareness that he has one chance and only one chance to communicate. Anyone with any experience in a radio or television newsroom knows how easy it is for listeners and viewers to misunderstand what they hear. The guiding principle, then, is to make broadcast copy understandable, to give the audience every opportunity to absorb what is said. The newspaper reader can return to a story or a troublesome phrase as many times as he must to make sense of it. The listener or viewer has no such luxury. His only recourse, if he cares that deeply, is to call and ask to have the item read back or explained, which, if it happens with any regularity, should be a clue to any broadcaster that he just is not getting through to his audience. The broadcaster should read over what is written to make absolutely certain that he has said what he wanted to say in direct, clear and completely understandable words.

These requirements hold just as true when pictures are added to a broadcast. Sometimes a picture helps to explain a story and at other times the picture itself needs some explaining. The television newsman must sharpen his sense of picture usage on the basis of understandability. Some of the techniques of doing that are dealt with later at greater length.

INFLECTION

While the broadcast journalist is at something of a disadvantage by the requirement associated with one-shot communication, there is something of a lovely, life-type balance injected by the fact that he has the compensating advantage of a marvelous tool to help him make himself understood. That instrument, of course, is his voice. Once again, an alert student must be impressed by the way each newscaster uses his voice. The professional broadcaster understands how to come to a complete stop between unrelated items. The chief requirement of broadcast copy is that it must flow in such a way that the broadcaster can punctuate it with his voice. The voice runs downhill to put the period at the end of a sentence. It climbs uphill again as the broadcaster launches into a new sentence, and carries a bit more of a push as he "punches" or emphasizes a key word or phrase. The voice drops off ever so slightly to insert the commas around a clause. The experienced broadcaster, like any good actor or orator, knows what he can do with his voice. If he writes his own copy, he can build his vocal style into that copy. If he reads copy others have written for him, he must allow time to go over the material carefully. A system of marking copy so as to get the most out of it is discussed and illustrated in the next chapter.

As is the case with any good thing, there is a danger of overdoing it with inflection. The newscaster is not giving a poetic or dramatic reading, and must not permit himself to be carried away. He must make his voice assist his mind in the act of communication. It is another of the subjective aspects of journalism in which taste is refined by experience.

WRITING ALOUD

Because of the vocal requirements of broadcast journalism, the casual visitor to an active newsroom might think he'd stumbled into some sort of Babel. Long ago, both broadcasters and those who write for broadcasters realized that copy should be read aloud as it is written. What better way could there be to check whether or not a pet phrase or sentence actually will "play" on air, or read properly, than to try it out at the typewriter in a sort of stage whisper. This is the sure way to reveal some clumsy grammatical construction or turn of phrase. If you can't get your tongue around a sentence, how can you expect to communicate thought with that particular way of expressing it? Happily, there ordinarily are infinite ways to say the same thing. It sometimes takes more than just a little thought to express something particularly well, but the effort can be immensely satisfying.

The technique of "writing aloud," while producing a one-language sort of Babel, also will demonstrate quickly several basic concepts of writing for the ear. First of all, the short sentences are easiest to read and to make others understand. Similarly, short, active words usually do a better job than long ones in conveying meaning audibly. Clauses can readily get the broadcaster into trouble and when they must be used they should be kept to as few words as possible. It stands to reason that a lengthy clause usually separates the subject and predicate by such a distance that the listener becomes lost in a jumble of words, even if the broadcaster can manage to find his way through the mess. Therefore, the broadcaster should try out as many different ways to say things as he can think of and eliminate the difficult, then learn to rely on those constructions he can articulate easily.

Of the three primary media for news dissemination, newspapers, radio and television, radio is the most demanding in point of understandability. Newspapers can be re-read. Television ordinarily reinforces the word with a picture. The radio newscaster must rely on his own ability to explain complex matters, to paint word pictures, and to create interesting ways to tell the news.

THE ELEMENT OF REPETITION

The need to gear the listener to what is coming was recognized long ago by radio newsmen. They evolved a formula of three parts: 1) tell the listener he's about to be told something; 2) tell him, and 3) tell him that you've told him. This time-honored formula often results in something like this:

A SURPRISE ANNOUNCEMENT THIS MORNING FROM THE WHITE HOUSE.

PRESIDENT MITCHELL DISCLOSES THAT HE WILL LEAVE TOMORROW FOR A VISIT TO FIVE WEST EUROPEAN NATIONS. HE WILL MEET WITH THE LEADERS OF BRITAIN, FRANCE, WEST GER- MANY AND ITALY.

A PRESIDENTIAL JOURNEY LIKE THIS HAD BEEN EXPECTED SOMETIME SOON, BUT MISTER MITCHELL NOW SPRINGS A SURPRISE WITH THE WORD HE'll GO TO WESTERN EUROPE TOMORROW.

It is an exaggeration to repeat so much in such a short item, but the principle should be clear. Again, it boils down to a question of style. Some newscasters feel their listeners are able to comprehend what they say with no difficulty and thus allow little of their air time to be spent in repetition. Others devise variations of their own on the old formula, perhaps "teeing up" a particular item that calls for something more than normal concentration, or else "buttoning" such a news story with a summary phrase or sentence. This is a decision that must be made by the individual newscaster on the basis of his own experience.

"PLAYING" A NEWS STORY

Even before the newscaster approaches his typewriter, he must decide how to "play" or treat the news story he is about to write. The decision initially involves a consideration of the kind of story it is: complex, tragic, serious, funny or whatever. Beyond that, the newscaster always is searching for some way to "freshen" the item. If a major news story has been worked hard for several hours during the day he might try to update it by leading with what is expected to happen tomorrow, if indeed there is a clear indication of that. Radio news, especially, is a "now" medium that looks constantly ahead and only rarely back as far as yesterday. Still another key consideration is how much time the newscaster can devote to an item and yet keep it in proper relationship to the other news of the day. Here, too, there usually is wide latitude within the boundaries of valid news judgment. The essence of some news stories can be told in one sentence, while others take some explaining.

Some newscasters like to lump news by geography; that is, to keep local, national and international news items bunched together within those categories. Others prefer to link items more or less by subject matter. Some newscasters display an almost evil sort of genius in "bridging" from one item to the next regardless of whether or not there is any sort of natural relationship. The practice of "wrestling" items together can produce some wildly imaginative constructions and it has come to be looked upon as totally unnecessary. Most professional newscasters today see greater merit in the technique of coming to a dead stop at the end of an item, taking a pause and moving right on to another, unrelated subject. The main point is that hard and fast rules for building a newscast or handling an individual news story do not exist. The construction is as much an offshoot of the broadcaster's own style as that style is the product of his education and experience, plus the professional development of his sense of news values. By and large, if the message comes through, it is a combination of good planning of the newscast, good writing and good delivery. Ordinarily, if the newscaster is falling down in any of these categories, he will hear about it soon enough from the news director, the station manager or some similarly "put out" listener, or possibly all three!

Still another basic factor in the decision of how to "play" a story is the consideration of whether it is for network or local use. For the network, naturally, the national approach to any item is desired. The newscaster on a local station should seek out the regional, state and local angles, if any, in a story. The newscaster for a network affiliate who takes the air either immediately before or after a network newscast certainly will concentrate on the local news. He should try, also, to develop the local angle of any national or even international story if indeed there are such angles. Sometimes it is wise and helpful for the local newscaster to make a telephone check with network news headquarters to discover how he can dovetail his coverage with the national angles of that particular story.

At this point, it might be helpful to take a basic kind of story that is handled by a wire service and show the different ways it would be handled by a network and a local radio station and also the ways the story might be updated.

First, the wire service copy:

WASHINGTON (API)—PRESIDENT MITCHELL, RETURNING TO WASHINGTON FROM HIS MICHIGAN VACATION HOME TONIGHT WAS UNDISTURBED BY A SUDDEN DIP WHICH TOSSED AIR FORCE ONE AROUND AND JARRED OTHER PASSENGERS.

THREE CREW MEMBERS WERE SHAKEN UP WHEN THE PRESIDENTIAL JET ENCOUNTERED THE TURBULENCE NEAR DETROIT, BUT UP FRONT MISTER MITCHELL WAS STRAPPED INTO HIS SEAT TALKING TO AN AIDE, NEWS SECRETARY ROBERT STOUGHTON SAID.

MISTER MITCHELL RETURNED TO THE WHITE HOUSE AT 9:22 PM, EST, FROM THE UPPER PENINSULA, WHERE HE HAD BEEN RESTING AFTER A STRENUOUS WIND-UP WEEK OF CONGRESS.

THE PRESIDENT LEAVES TOMORROW FOR PARIS AND FOUR OTHER WEST EUROPEAN CITIES.

WHILE STILL IN MICHIGAN, STOUGHTON SAID, MISTER MITCHELL CONFERRED ON THE TELEPHONE WITH GOVERNOR GEORGE NYE OF

NEW YORK, SLIGHTLY DELAYING THE TAKE-OFF
FOR WASHINGTON. STOUGHTON SAID NYE HAD
TRIED TO REACH MISTER MITCHELL AND THE
PRESIDENT RETURNED THE CALL. THEY WILL BE
GETTING TOGETHER WHEN THE GOVERNOR
COMES TO WASHINGTON TO MEET WITH THE NEW
YORK STATE CONGRESSIONAL DELEGATION NEXT
WEEK, AFTER THE PRESIDENT RETURNS FROM
EUROPE. STOUGHTON SAID THE PRESIDENT AND
THE GOVERNOR WILL BE TALKING ABOUT
FEDERAL-STATE RELATIONSHIPS AND
ESPECIALLY NYE'S EFFORT TO EASE HIS STATE'S
TAX BURDEN WITH MORE FEDERAL AID.

CR1024PES NOV 10

The above artificial example runs just short of 200 words.
The average newscaster probably could read it in 50 seconds
to a minute or so. Wire service copy always should be
rewritten for air, especially those "A" wire stories that so
obviously are structured for newspaper use. Another factor
that should be considered is the fact that the above news item
is less than earth-shaking in importance. It is the sort of thing
a wire service almost is duty-bound to report for the record.
Unless a radio newscaster is desperate to fill time, he almost
certainly would strip away the infinite detail reported. For
purposes of illustration, let's say the network newscaster had
planned his production and allowed 15 seconds for this particular item. He might handle it like this:

PRESIDENT MITCHELL TOOK A BIT OF A BUF-
FETING TONIGHT AS HE RETURNED TO
WASHINGTON. ON THE FLIGHT FROM HIS
VACATION HOME IN MICHIGAN, AIR FORCE ONE
RAN INTO SOME HEAVY WEATHER. THREE
CREWMEN WERE SHAKEN UP, BUT THE
PRESIDENT WAS ALL RIGHT. HE TAKES OFF
TOMORROW FOR A TOUR OF WESTERN EUROPE.

That item would hold up for one network newscast, but
network radio news is characterized, mainly, by frequent
service, which means at least one newscast per hour
throughout most of the broadcast day. Thus, when the
newscaster who delivered the above item comes up for his
second newscast of the night, he is going to have to update the

story, or rewrite it and freshen it. Obviously, if the wire story moved late at night, and the sign-off time at the end of the item says it cleared the wire at 10:24 PM, EST, there's little likelihood that the White House would release anything further on the incident in the plane or any further news at that hour, barring some major new development. In all probability, the White House news official on duty would have announced that "the lid" was on for the night, which is the jargon for no more news expected, and the newscaster is left to work within the framework of the story as it was sent originally. In this case, there's an obvious new tack:

PRESIDENT MITCHELL TAKES OFF TOMORROW ON A TOUR OF WESTERN EUROPE. AS HE RETURNED TO WASHINGTON TONIGHT FROM HIS VACATION HOME IN MICHIGAN, MISTER MITCHELL ESCAPED INJURY AS HIS JET RAN INTO HEAVY WEATHER. THREE CREWMEN WERE SHAKEN UP.

To demonstrate quite a different approach to the same basic story, let's invent a situation in which a radio newscaster at a station in Albany, N.Y., is looking for material to fill his 11 PM broadcast. As the item clears the wire, he finds he has 30 seconds open. His approach could be something like this:

PRESIDENT MITCHELL RETURNED TO WASHINGTON TONIGHT AFTER A TELEPHONE CHAT WITH NEW YORK'S GOVERNOR GEORGE NYE. THE PAIR MADE AN APPOINTMENT TO MEET AT THE WHITE HOUSE NEXT WEEK, AFTER MISTER MITCHELL RETURNS FROM A TOUR OF WESTERN EUROPE. GOVERNOR NYE IS TRYING TO PRY MORE FEDERAL FUNDS OUT OF WASHINGTON TO EASE THE TAX BURDEN IN THIS STATE.

FOR HIS PART, PRESIDENT MITCHELL TOOK A BUFFETING WHEN HIS JET RAN INTO HEAVY WINDS ON THE TRIP FROM THE VACATION WHITE HOUSE IN MICHIGAN. THREE CREWMEN WERE SHAKEN UP, BUT THE PRESIDENT WAS UN-HARMED.

For the Albany broadcaster, one obvious update for his midnight newscast could be that Governor Nye is going to meet with President Mitchell next week. After leading with that information, he can back into the other pertinent details he needs to fill however much time he allows for the item.

Similarly, if the Albany newscaster found he had only 15 seconds to tell the story, he simply would have to drop more and more detail to get his item down to size. It is the frustration of broadcast journalists that they frequently don't have the time they need to give a story adequate treatment. Time requirements pose many challenges to newscasters to say as much as they can about a story and say it well no matter how inadequate they feel the allotted time is. In this example, a 15-second local version might take this form:

GOVERNOR GEORGE NYE WILL OUTLINE NEW YORK'S TAX PROBLEMS TO PRESIDENT MITCHELL NEXT WEEK. THE DATE WAS ARRANGED BY PHONE TONIGHT, JUST BEFORE THE PRESIDENT FLEW BACK TO WASHINGTON FROM HIS VACATION HOME IN MICHIGAN. MISTER MITCHELL LEAVES TOMORROW ON A TOUR OF EUROPE.

There are many ways to update news stories. Sometimes a new lead produced by the wire service will come to the rescue of the newscaster struggling against a deadline. Often, in the case of local news, the newscaster may have to take time to make a few telephone calls to dig out a fresh angle. This is another area in which an imaginative approach can move a story along in time and information content. The broadcast journalist must always be on the alert to help his product in this way.

THE PRESENT TENSE

Again, it is impossible to put too much stress on broadcast journalism's advantage of absolute immediacy. Because of this, the practice arose in radio news, and has been carried over into television, where writers try to put stories in the present tense. The practice serves more of a useful purpose in radio because of the greater frequency of news broadcasts. For stations that chew up news at a rapid rate, there is merit in trying to freshen a story by digging out the angle that legitimately can be told in the present tense. Thus, after a local fire has been reported for several hours, for instance, the newscaster picking up that story might try an approach like this:

FIREMEN STILL ARE SIFTING THROUGH THE RUBBLE OF GREEN'S DEPARTMENT STORE. THEY'RE TRYING TO FIND OUT WHAT CAUSED THE FIRE THAT DESTROYED THE BUILDING THIS MORNING.

Constant updating is the duty of the newscaster who wants to make the best use of his medium for fast communication.

SOME HELPFUL HINTS

When at last all the preparations are out of the way and the newscaster actually is ready to write, there are some time-tested practices he can follow to make his task easier. First of all, it is good practice to type the script with triple spacing between lines. It is easier to read and there is room for edits that are easily understood at a glance. Whether the newscaster or an editor or someone else in authority pens in a change, it should be printed neatly. The danger here is obvious.

It is wise to write each individual item on a separate page. The advantage becomes obvious when a story changes near air time and must be rewritten. Instead of having to cut copy

Typical large-city or network radio, viewed from the broadcaster's position. The control room is located beyond the plate glass window.

when the item in question is somewhere near the middle of the script, the broadcaster simply drops the page, retypes it and slips it back into its proper place. In this regard, it also is practical to number pages in the order in which they will be delivered. If last-minute additions become necessary, they can be put into proper place by combining numerals and letters.

Some newscasters prefer to hold the script in hand behind of the microphone as they broadcast. Others simply position the microphone so as to leave enough room to place the script on the desk before them. This is a matter of individual comfort. As a story is read, some newscasters simply drop the page of copy to the floor; others merely turn it over, face down, nearby. The chief factor is the newscaster's own preference, recognizing that the microphone is a sensitive instrument and often picks up the sound of a newscaster handling his script.

It is to be expected that experience will teach the newscaster to work better and quicker. As he writes more, he will take less time to produce his script. His day-to-day association with news and his own observations on the way it develops and flows should teach him how to improve his work habits. As his facility expands, however, it remains important for him to budget enough time for both preparation and rehearsal and especially to avoid unnecessary pressure. The business of news provides more than enough excitement and last-minute changes—no extra tension is needed. The newscaster does himself a favor every time he plans well enough to allow himself time to **walk** into the studio instead of running into it. Try it for yourself if you need a demonstration of how one's ability to read aloud is diminished by a sprint and the shortened breath that results from even a short dash. Neither the author nor anyone else who saw it ever will forget the scene when a nationally-known newscaster played things just too close to the deadline and dashed into the studio only to knock his hand against the door and see his script fly into the air and float down about him in disarray just as the horrified staff announcer was introducing him.

A MATTER OF STYLE

It would be wrong to end any discussion of writing for broadcast without making a few important points about writing style. Most wire service copy is cluttered with cliches. In large part, this is so because wire service writers are put under enormous pressure to move a lot of copy. Much the same danger faces many radio and television newsmen, especially in situations where their on-the-air load is heavy. Obviously, in these situations, scripts must be hammered out quickly, with little time for thought and less for polished writing. It is to the credit of any radio or television station or network if that organization employs enough broadcasters to allow each individual enough time to write clear, crisp copy and lace it with examples of interesting ways to say something.

CBS News Correspondent John Hart and Harry Reasoner, formerly of CBS News and now co-anchor with Howard K. Smith of the ABC Evening News, are two whose avoidance of the cliche has helped to make them the interesting and efficient newscasters they are on both radio and television. Anyone who ever has written for Reasoner has been gently but positively informed of his intolerance for overworked phrases. He doesn't write them for himself and expects those who do write for him to spare him the torture of an "oil rich sheikdom of Kuwait" or similar phrases and descriptions so common to wire service output. Hart's directions to his writers begin with the instruction to try to say everything in a way that it's never been said before and Hart does just that in the copy he writes for himself.

The English language is a marvelously broad and flexible means of communication. For the broadcast journalist, the language and the radio and television media mesh most effectively when the newscaster learns how to approach his listeners and viewers in a conversational way. He listens to the ways people speak and understands the rhythms that run through a conversation. In itself, this is a fascinating study and it can make a broadcaster into a communicator.

CHAPTER 5

Marking & Timing the Script

For the professional broadcaster, the aim every time he goes on the air is to deliver as nearly perfect a report as he can. As with any other endeavor, the fineness of the finished product depends on proper preparation. Thus, for the newscaster, there are two more basic steps before going on air: marking, or "road mapping," the copy and timing it with infinite care.

In the case of the newscaster who does not write his own copy, it is vital that he goes over the script carefully to familiarize himself with its contents. Most newscasters devise a system of marking their copy for ease of reading and authoritative delivery. The simpler the system the more helpful it will be in assisting the broadcaster to put emphasis in the proper places, to pace himself, and to breathe in a normal, relaxed way and not have to gulp for air at the end of a sentence. Generally, the technique of marking a script involves reading the copy aloud, which provides a double check for awkward sentence construction or such hazards as an alliteration that might have crept unintentionally into the copy in the writing stage. The newscaster has enough to think about on the air without getting himself trapped, and careful copy marking will help him avoid the pitfalls.

The veteran American Broadcasting Company newscaster, Don Gardiner, long ago developed a marking system that he feels gives him a decided boost. The point of his system, he says, is to assist the mind and the eye as aids to voicing a clearly understood newscast. As Gardiner puts it: "In driving, it's easier to follow a road map that has been marked with the route beforehand, and in reading copy it follows that it should be easier to read if the copy has been marked. Marks placed in the copy beforehand remind you where the important parts of a story are. They indicate how to phrase the sentence to get the most meaning out of it, where to pause, and where pitfalls in language or pronunciation are."

Gardiner's script marking system boils down to eight key symbols:

1. The beginning of an independent item is marked⌊//⌋. It indicates a new story, or a new thought.

Don Gardiner at his ABC microphone.

2. Underlining with a <u>single line</u> points up an important word or phrase. A <u>double line</u> is used to denote something that merits even more emphasis, or "punching up."

3. A slanted line / denotes the end of a phrase and suggests a separation from what follows or an opportunity to take a breath in a natural break.

4. Double slanted lines // put a definite end to a story or indicate an end to that phase of a story with another facet to follow.

5. A wavy line beneath a word or phrase is a reminder that the word or phrase lends itself to a slight bit of color or dramatization.

6. When a word, phrase or even a sentence has been cut, a curved line is carried ~~is carried~~ from the pick up point back to the point where omission begins to lead the eye over the dropped material.

7. Parentheses ( ) are used to indicate a phrase of lesser value and entire items that are optional and could be dropped for time purposes.

8. Finally, when a word or phrase is written into the script ∧ *by hand* a bracket and insert caret help the eye put the additional material in its proper place.

Don Gardiner's experience in newscasting has taught him to mark copy automatically, and always on the first reading. Indeed, he says marking has become so much second nature to him that even when a bulletin is rushed to him while he is on the air, he marks it as he reads it! His system of "road mapping" his copy is illustrated in the following sample 5-minute newscast:

GOOD MORNING FROM THE A.B.C. NEWSROOM IN NEW YORK.

THIS IS DON GARDINER WITH THE TEN O'CLOCK REPORT.

FIRST, ~~A LOOK AT~~ THE HEADLINES: ⟶

A PRESIDENTIAL JOURNEY IS ANNOUNCED. DESTINATION: WESTERN EUROPE/..

THE U.S. SENATE NEARS A FINAL VOTE ON THE HISTORIC DISARMAMENT TREATY/.

TWO CALIFORNIA DOCTORS ARE HONORED FOR CANCER RESEARCH/

....AND, TORNADOES AND HEAVY WEATHER HIT THE SOUTH./

THE DETAILS ON THESE AND OTHER TOP STORIES OF THE HOUR IN A MOMENT:// (COMMERCIAL 1:00)

//NOW, THE NEWS IN DETAIL:

THE WHITE HOUSE ANNOUNCED THIS MORNING/THAT PRESIDENT MITCHELL WILL LEAVE TOMORROW/FOR A QUICK VISIT TO FIVE WEST EUROPEAN NATIONS. THE TRIP,(ITSELF,) IS NO SURPRISE/..JUST THE TIMING OF IT. MISTER MITCHELL WASN'T EXPECTED TO LEAVE UNTIL NEXT WEEK/FOR TALKS WITH THE LEADERS OF BRITAIN,/ BELGIUM,/ FRANCE,/ WEST GERMANY/ AND ITALY.

THE WHITE HOUSE WON'T COMMENT, (OF COURSE) BUT SOURCES IN WASHINGTON SAY/THE TIMING OF THE PRESIDENTIAL TRIP INDICATES THAT MISTER MITCHELL NOW EXPECTS SWIFT/ SENATE APPROVAL OF THE LONG-DEBATE DISARMAMENT TREATY.

THAT AGREEMENT COMMITTING THE "SUPERPOWERS" TO A SHARP CUTBACK IN ARMS PRODUCTION/COMES UP FOR A VOTE/WHEN THE SENATE MEETS AT NOON. A TWO-THIRDS MAJORITY VOTE IS REQUIRED FOR APPROVAL.

THE agreement VOTE WOULD BE A LANDMARK IN DIPLOMATIC HISTORY AND WOULD CLIMAX A FIVE-YEAR EFFORT TO LINK THE UNITED STATES,/ THE SOVIET UNION/BRITAIN/AND FRANCE/IN AN AGREEMENT TO LIMIT THEIR OUTPUT OF NUCLEAR AND CONVENTIONAL WEAPONS.

BRITAIN AND FRANCE ALREADY HAVE GRANTED PARLIAMENTARY APPROVAL TO THE TREATY. ACTION IN MOSCOW AND WASHINGTON IS NOW NEARING COMPLETION.

PRESIDENT MITCHELL HAD PROMISED TO CONSULT WITH THE NATION'S TOP ALLIES/ON——→

FUTURE DISARMAMENT PLANS/ AS SOON AS A FAVORABLE VOTE IN THE SENATE ~~WAS~~ *is* ASSURED.

BEFORE HE TAKES OFF TOMORROW FOR LONDON/ PRESIDENT MITCHELL/ MUST SETTLE A FINANCIAL SQUABBLE WITHIN HIS AD-MINISTRATION. TREASURY SECRETARY CHARLES ALEXANDER IS PRESSING FOR A ROLLBACK OF ~~EIGHT HUNDRED AND TWENTY-FIVE~~ *825* MILLION DOLLARS IN FEDERAL AID/ TO HIGHER EDUCATION IN THE NEXT FISCAL YEAR. THE SECRETARY OF HEALTH, EDUCATION AND WELFARE, ALBERT IGNATIUS/ SAYS THE MONEY IS A TOP PRIORITY ITEM/ AND ~~VOWS~~ *says* HE'LL FIGHT TO KEEP IT. PRESIDENT MITCHELL HAS CALLED ~~BOTH CABINET OFFICERS~~ *education and treasury officials* IN FOR A FINAL DISCUSSION THIS AFTERNOON.//

TWO BIOCHEMISTS/ ASSOCIATED WITH THE UNIVERSITY OF CALIFORNIA/ TODAY WERE DECLARED WINNERS/ OF THIS YEAR'S FIFTY-THOUSAND DOLLAR OLIVER FOUNDATION PRIZE FOR CANCER RESEARCH. SHARING THIS AWARD/ ARE DOCTORS PHILIP EVERS AND SIGMUND SCH-MIDT. THEY WERE CITED FOR MICROSCOPIC STUDIES/ THAT SHED NEW LIGHT ON THE PROCESS OF METASTASIS. THAT'S THE WAY CANCER CAN FORM NEW GROWTHS IN PARTS OF THE BODY/ FAR FROM THE ORIGINAL SITE. *of a tumor.*//

DOWN SOUTH/ SOME WILD WEATHER. THAT STORY AFTER THIS MESSAGE.// (COMMERCIAL :30)

TORNADOES STRUCK LATE LAST NIGHT/ IN WIDELY-SEPARATED PARTS OF FLORIDA. ONE TWISTER TOUCHED DOWN AT IMMOKALEE, (SOUTHEAST OF FORT MYERS) AND ANOTHER HIT PALATKA (IN THE NORTHEASTERN PART OF THE STATE.) DAMAGE WAS EXTENSIVE IN BOTH PLACES...BUT NO DEATHS OR INJURIES ~~WERE~~ *are* REPORTED.

AT THE SAME TIME,/ TORRENTIAL RAINS LASHED PARTS OF ALABAMA AND GEORGIA,/ BRINGING HIGHWAY TRAVEL ALMOST TO A STANDSTILL. CLEARING WEATHER ~~IS~~ *is* FORECAST FOR TODAY.//

THE REST OF THE UNITED STATES IS EN-JOYING GENERALLY CLEAR/ MILD WEATHER THIS MORNING. THE ONLY EXCEPTION IS THE PACIFIC ⟶

NORTHWEST, / WHERE RAIN AND FOG ~~WERE~~ *are*/
PREDICTED ~~IN~~ *for* THE ~~FORENOON HOURS~~ *morning*//
||THAT'S THE NEWS FOR NOW. THIS IS DON
GARDINER REPORTING FROM THE XXX A.B.C.
NEWSROOM IN NEW YORK. GOOD BYE AND HAVE A
GOOD DAY!//

Don Gardiner's illustration provides several other practical considerations regarding broadcast copy. Numbers and statistics play an important part in news, and the newsman must soon decide for himself how best to handle them. For one individual, it is easier both to read and to time numerals that are written out completely, so that eight-hundred-and-twenty-five-million dollars is his style. In Gardiner's case, he struck out the spelled out figure and converted it into 825-million dollars and yet, just a few lines later, let fifty-thousand stand. For him, then, it is easier to grasp the sight of numerals in series when the figures are used and a rounded figure when spelled out. Still another newscaster might find his eye easily takes in the figures, and he prefers to use it as 825,000,000 dollars. The latter version is rare, however, and leaves more room than most individuals need for error.

Few newsmen are such proficient typists that they can rattle off clean copy regularly. This is unimportant. What is important, however, is the manner in which the "typos" or mistakes are cleaned up. It is far more distracting than helpful, for instance, to try to clean up a letter within a word. When one or two letters are missing or out of place it is better to strike over the entire word and pen it in properly. By the same token, it is aggravating to see a word broken at the end of a line or, far worse, to another page. A much wiser and more helpful practice is just to hold the entire word off until the next line or page and keep it intact.

Notice that Don Gardiner places an arrow at the bottom of a page when the item carries over to the next page. This is another way of helping the eye move easily over the copy.

BREATHING FOR BROADCAST

The other major value of a good marking system is the help it provides in pacing a newscast and telling the broadcaster where he can pause naturally to breathe. With his typically professional understatement, Don Gardiner says that the trick in breathing for broadcast is to make sure you have some breath left when you get to the end of a sentence or item. Inexperienced broadcasters tend to take short, choppy breaths or else often gulp for air in the middle of a sentence. Listening to tape playbacks should soon convince them there's a better way, which involves breathing deeply from the diaphragm, that large muscle which separates the chest from the abdomen. The practice of breathing from the diaphragm gives the broadcaster greater speaking endurance and control. The practice of inhaling through the nose also is wise in that it helps to avoid the sound of air gulping, which microphones amplify to the point of annoyance.

The pattern of breathing for broadcast should be the same as in conversational speech in which you breathe in between phrases and sentences. A speaker can put added emphasis into his delivery by biting off an entire short sentence or collection of phrases in one breath. Proper "road mapping" can get the newscaster safely through an inordinately long sentence, if one should creep into the script, but it is better to chop the sentence down during the marking session. Often it will be desirable for the newscaster to alter his normal breathing pattern to change or give new emphasis to a news story that calls for special treatment. Perhaps the item would benefit by a staccato sort of reading. This is accomplished by taking frequent short breaths. On the other hand, if called upon within the body of a newscast to read an excerpt of poetry, the broadcaster might discover that the same breath can carry him over four or five lines.

It is during the marking run through that the newscaster should nail down his pacing, or the speed with which he will deliver each item. Obviously, he develops a "feel" for the story as he writes it. The type of story dictates the reading speed. An obituary or story of a tragedy, naturally, demands a slower pace and more somber tone. A happy, light story might suggest a speedier reading. A story containing many numerals requires the newscaster to slow his normal pace so the listener can hear and understand. As a general rule, it is wise to try to restrict the use of numbers to absolute essentials because the listener may have difficulty understanding them.

With the short 5-minute newscast, at least a degree of uniformity of pacing is required. Generally, the tendency is to try to pack in as many items as possible to give the newscast a quickened pace and to convey the feeling that a lot of news is being covered. This naturally cuts down the time for each item and the detail that often provides the cue for some sort of vocal variation.

TIMING THE SCRIPT

There is absolutely no escaping the basic fact that broadcasting is a business of minutes and seconds; that, in the end, the clock often determines what can be broadcast. For the newsman at the local, independent radio or television station, the restrictions may not be quite so rigid as they are in network operations, but they are there nonetheless and must be obeyed. When a newscaster is scheduled to go on air at such and such a time, he had just better be in front of the microphone or camera and be ready to go. It obviously is wise to be in the studio a few minutes before air time to get positioned comfortably and to be free for last-minute changes, voice level checks and microphone and camera placement. When the program schedule calls for the newscast to end, the newscaster should be ready to bring it to a conclusion.

In an independent operation, there is some leeway because the program origination is controlled right there at the station. If, for instance, a radio newscast leads into a disc jockey show, the latter can be held up until the newscast is concluded. Similarly, a local television station can squeeze a few seconds here and there. Life can be made easier for everybody, however, if newscasters and all other performers make it standard operating procedure to confine themselves to scheduled times.

The newscaster in the network operation always has labored under the threat of being cut off the air if he ran more than about five seconds over his allotted time. In the old days, it was a human decision to clip a performer or newscaster who violated the time limitation. Today, whatever leeway resulted from human involvement is gone because the networks for the most part are controlled, time wise, by computers so that the perhaps hundreds of affiliated radio or television stations across the nation get the network feed at the time they expect to get it.

Still another factor to be considered in timing a script is the inclusion and placement of commercials or promotional announcements. Ordinarily, advertising agencies and sponsors either buy a particular newscast outright or buy "spot" announcements, or individual commercials running usually to 30 seconds or one minute within the body of a newscast. The buyer might want his commercial to be aired at a particular time, although in the more routine situation it is specified that the commercial go on the air in the first, second or whatever position is desired. Whatever the case, it falls to the radio newscaster to find out what announcements are included in his production. In the case of participating network programs, in which local affiliates sell local commercials and cut away from the network for a prescribed time, the newscaster must time his copy to the precise second. Whatever the commercial arrangement, the newscaster should handle it with glee: the commercials pay his fee!

THE LINE COUNT

It would be impractical for the newscaster to time each story with a stopwatch as he writes it. The problem is obviated by the long standing practice of counting lines. Most radio newscasters read about 15 full lines of typewritten copy in a minute and it is a simple matter to use a stopwatch to determine the exact reading speed. When the reading speed has been determined, it is no great trick to gauge the development of a newscast. Some newscasters count the lines of each story. Others who put more than one item on a page count lines page by page. For example, if he is preparing a five-minute newscast and knows that his reading speed is 15 lines per minute, simple arithmetic decrees that 75 lines of copy will do the job. Then, the newscaster checks the program schedule and learns that, on that particular day, there will be one one-minute and one 30-second commercial within his newscast, so that eliminates 23 lines (15 for the one-minute commercial and a generous eight lines instead of seven and a half for the 30-second commercial). This leaves him with 52 lines, and the standard opening and closing might cut the total by, say, another four lines, leaving him 48 lines of copy to write.

Bear in mind that the line count serves only as a preliminary guide and not a final timing. That comes later. When the newscaster has determined how many lines he needs, he can calculate how many stories he can get into the production and roughly how many lines he can give to each story. It might be that he knows he wants to treat eight stories of more or less equal importance which, at 48 lines, breaks down to about six lines per item. More realistically, he probably will have two or three items of greater significance and several of lesser importance, and the available lines will be distributed according to his news judgment.

STOPWATCH TIMING AND BACK-TIMING

When all the copy is written, edited and "road mapped" and the time for the broadcast nears, the newscaster should prepare himself more accurately with a stopwatch timing of his production. Here, too, techniques vary from individual to individual. One broadcaster will be more comfortable by writing down the seconds, or minutes and seconds, consumed cumulatively on the watch at the end of each full page of copy. Another will mark time at the end of each item. Someone else might mark to the clock, itself, so that if he is taking air at eight o'clock, he will write down where in relation to the exact hour he should be at any given point. The system itself is not the important thing, but rather that some helpful, precise way is developed to time a newscast. Then, when a full stopwatch timing has been done, there remains one final check to make certain the production will get off the air at the right time.

CBS News Correspondent Allan Jackson is another veteran broadcaster whose painstaking attention to every

CBS newscaster Allan Jackson. (Courtesy Norman Goldman)

detail of his productions is exemplified by the meticulous way he times them. Jackson has been engaged in broadcasting long enough that he could take air comfortably with only a line count, but his professional attitude requires him to check and double check. It is not difficult to see how, with the preparations he makes, Jackson is as regular as the clock, itself.

In addition to his regular newscasts, Allan Jackson writes and broadcasts a news background program called "The Morning Report" every Monday through Saturday on the CBS Radio Network. He and the management were kind enough to grant permission to reprint a copy of one of Jackson's original scripts to demonstrate his timing techniques. "The Morning Report" runs for a total of four minutes and 30 seconds, including commercials. It opens with a musical identification and closes with a musical signature that is faded in during the sign-off. On New Year's morning, 1970, Allan Jackson broadcast the following:

The Morning Report...I'm Allan Jackson—CBS

News, N.Y.

The new decade is here—~~XXXXX~~ *the* sound of the

seventies is upon us —/even IF, to many, the

SOUND — at whatever level — is much too high — in

these first ~~XXXXXXX~~ hours ~~XXXXXXXX~~ *after* a welcoming

celebration. A look at the new ~~XXX~~ year — and its

~~XXX~~ offerings — in a moment.

(Commercial)

There's a little <u>bit</u>/for quite a few in the

new year/that is unfolding as the sun rises this

morning. For the twenty-five million <u>senior</u> citizens of the country —there's a pay raise, of sorts, to <u>look</u> forward to —the <u>fifteen percent</u> hike in social security benefits. For taxpayers — <u>generally</u> —there are some small gifts in the offing from the tax reform bill *signed* by the president. For the <u>young</u> men of the nation, there's the <u>prospect</u> of a more equitable military draft system/— *in* the <u>lottery</u> method <u>of</u> selecting draftees *which* becomes effective today — even though the <u>first drawing</u> of <u>numbers</u> has already been held.

For the <u>minority</u> members of the population, there's an improved housing outlook as of today —for the <u>1968</u> Open Housing Law now becomes fully effective — meaning that *some* thirty-four million single-family homes are being added to the apartments, and other dwellings already covered by the first two stages of this federal fair housing law.

In other areas, the State of California breaks some new ground as of this New Year's day. It is doing away with the <u>term</u>

"divorce" / and replacing it with the legal phrase "dissolution of marriage." Among its more revolutionary aspects / — the new law eliminates the idea of guilt / — and divorce, (in California anyway —) ceases to be an adversary action before the courts. The co-author of the law —/ state senator Donald Grunsky says — "we're not trying to make divorce easier — we're ~~xxx~~ simply trying to take the acrimony out of it."

And —of course — on more mundane matters — the new year means — election years / and a campaign ahead for a lot of politicans. All members of the House of Representatives —/ and a third of the Senate and about three-fourths of the *governors* ~~goornors~~ ·/ are up for re-election in this *new* ~~near~~ year of 1970 —/ and many of them— are already running.

Now this message:

(commercial)

I'm Allan Jackson — This has been The Morning Report...on CBS Radio.

Allan Jackson is a staunch defender and able practitioner of the art of writing "hear" copy; that is, copy that is written for someone else's ear and not his eye. His words are chosen carefully to convey meaning precisely and understandably. He shuns the old practice of putting verbal quotation marks around excerpts from someone else's words and, instead, uses his own vocal inflection to do that job. Jackson's own simplified marking system helps him get the most effective reading possible and by his careful timing· he makes certain that what he has written and rehearsed will get on the air. In the lower right-hand corner of each page of script, Jackson jots down the number of full lines, compensating where necessary for partial lines. Optional material, full sentences or phrases that can be dropped are bracketed and not considered in the line count.

A fully-sponsored "Morning Report" includes a 30-second commercial in the first position that follows one quick paragraph to introduce the subject, and a one-minute commercial when the report is complete and just before the sign-off. Thus, the total air time of 4 minutes and 30 seconds is cut to 3 minutes of copy, less another 15 seconds that include 5 seconds for the music and opening and 10 seconds for the sign-off and signature music. In total, then, the example contains just about 2 minutes and 45 seconds of copy to be read by the broadcaster. Long experience has taught Jackson that he needs 42 lines for a fully-sponsored "Morning Report." The line count is made and marked as each page comes out of the typewriter, serving as a constant guide regarding the amount of copy and time he has left to say what he wants to say.

When he has written 42 lines, Jackson immediately goes back to edit his copy, cleaning up typos and marking the places he wants to pause to take a breath or to underscore some point of fact verbally. Actually, Jackson is reading all the time he is writing. He verbalizes phrases to make sure they sound well, often putting a word in capital letters if that word needs or lends itself to particular emphasis. Jackson also uses dashes to assist his distinctive reading style.

When the script has been written, edited and marked, Jackson gives it a complete read-through in a stage whisper, delivering it exactly as he will before the microphone. This time, however, his stopwatch is running. If a thought about the copy strikes him, he stops the watch, makes the addition, deletion or whatever, then proceeds from there, making note on the copy of the elapsed time. Thus, in the sample script, he has calculated that he should be out of the first commercial and into the body of the report at 55 seconds. He figures he should hit the word "population" on the second page at one-minute and 30-seconds into the production. His timing brings him to the start of his third page at two-minutes. Because of his original line count, he usually comes out close to the right time. If by some chance his timing is off, it usually is off only by a matter of a few seconds, something that can be adjusted by the addition or deletion of a line, or perhaps even a phrase.

Finally, and just for the insurance that meticulous professionals demand, Allan Jackson back-times his script. For his sign-off and the musical signature, Jackson needs ten seconds. Thus, he notes on the script that he must begin his sign-off at four-minutes and 20 seconds into the report. His final commercial runs one minute, and he notes that, to come out exactly on time, he must cue that commercial at three-minutes-and-twenty-seconds. He times his final paragraph and notes that it requires 18 seconds to read, a sign to him that he must have 18 seconds on the studio watch to hit the commercial cue on time. He times back some more to find out that he should have 33 seconds left on the watch when he reaches the word "ALTHOUGH" on page three, and back to the beginning of that paragraph, which he must hit with 50-seconds and back still further to the last sentence of the first paragraph, which he wants to reach with one-minute remaining to his commercial. Jackson makes it a practice to have the associate director, who sits with him in the studio to cue the engineer for music and commercials, show him a stopwatch with one-minute to the commercial. Thus, if everything is working the way it should, the associate director will show him the watch as he goes into that final sentence of the first paragraph on page three, beginning "The co-author of the law..."

This may all seem like a tremendous amount of work, but it isn't really. It gets to be second nature after a short while, and the results are well worth the effort. It is a common failing among broadcasters to read at two different speeds, at least. Often they will time something carefully in the newsroom or their office, then go on air and read at a faster or slower speed to create timing problems for themselves and anyone else involved in the production. The young broadcaster should strive to cultivate a uniform reading-timing system and learn how to back-time to save himself from having to rush through to the conclusion of a newscast or to slow down so noticeably that it becomes obvious to a listener or viewer that something has gone wrong.

PAD COPY AND OPTIONAL MATERIAL

Still another technique which has proven valuable by long usage is that of carrying some pad or fill copy along to the studio. What this means is that, in writing the newscast, the broadcaster simply selects an item or two of lesser importance and writes them for supplemental use if, for instance, he does pick up some time on air and finds himself running out of copy ahead of time. Conversely, it makes good sense to mark off an item or several sentences that can be dropped on the air if for one reason or another the newscaster finds himself running over.

CHAPTER 6

Use of Audio Tape

A major contribution to the reshaping the radio newscast in recent years has been the refinement of highly portable, highly sensitive, yet relatively inexpensive tape recording equipment. Time was in radio when tape recording a news event was a major production in its own right. Often, it required the presence of an audio engineer to lug a heavy recording instrument, to make certain it ran properly and to make the tape recording. In those days, the standard network practice was to make what amounts today to a high fidelity recording, using a tape speed of 15 inches per second (IPS). Today, anyone who operates a radio station, from the 250 watter on up, can afford to use tape in even the most limited sort of news operation. Now, it is almost standard operating procedure to equip radio reporters with pocket-sized tape recorders. The old standard of 15 IPS has been abandoned. In network operations, audio engineers still prefer to have the quality that can be reached with recordings made at 7½ inches per second, but 3¾ IPS is often considered broadcast quality and, in a pinch, 1⅞ IPS can be made to do or put through a conversion process to improve the quality.

In recent years, cartridge and cassette tapes have come along to make life easier for radio engineers and broadcasters who run their own equipment on the air. Cartridges and cassettes are made of plastic and contain a reel-to-reel or an endless length of audio tape. The advantage is that the tape doesn't have to be threaded onto a machine or handled at all. The case simply is slipped into a slot in an electronic device that cues the tape to the starting place automatically, plays it at the throw of a switch, then rewinds it once it has been played, thus relieving the operator of many chores.

With all the flexibility of audio tape, radio stations with a bent for news now make extensive use of taped actuality and voice reports or interviews with prominent figures and individuals who are involved in the developments of the day. Indeed, **Broadcasting Magazine** reports that more than 3,000 radio stations are "reaping the benefits of this trend toward

Reel-to-reel audio tape recording and playback machines.
(Courtesy Norman Goldman)

virtually instantaneous coverage with the sound of news as it is happening, from where it is happening." The stations include affiliates of the American Broadcasting Company, the Columbia Broadcasting System, Mutual and the National Broadcasting Company. These four major networks daily take in hundreds of "feeds" from their own reporters and from affiliated stations. They retain the right to select the best, most topical and most interesting of these offerings for their own broadcasting needs. Beyond that, they make closed-circuit "feeds" to all affiliates, providing them with choice selections that affiliates can use as they see fit. Moreover, specialized audio services such as UPI Audio Networik, Radio News International and Metromedia Radio News are selling their reports to stations. Other networks and group-owned facilities such as Capital Cities Broadcasting Corp., Triangle, Westinghouse, Storer and others have their own arrangements for gathering and distributing taped reports in keen competition that reflects the increasing importance of news in radio.

GETTING THE STORY ON AUDIO TAPE

With this constantly increasing demand for news coverage, more and more correspondents, reporters and stringers are in the field, at home and abroad, watching, filming, listening to and tape recording important events and interesting feature material. Major independent radio and television stations and groups assign trained personnel to special bureaus in Washington, where they "dig out" news stories, interviews and other information that is important to the listening areas they serve. It is common, also, for major independent stations to set up a bureau in the state capital for direct reports on developments in government that affect the local area.

In the case of the networks, this specialized coverage is multiplied many times over. The networks are responsible for extensive national and international coverage which is served to affiliated stations. This responsibility imposes a heavy manpower and financial burden of setting up bureaus in major cities and world capitals where news is likely to happen and from where reporters can quickly be moved to the scene of important news events.

For the radio news correspondent, audio coverage breaks down into three chief categories: 1) taped "actuality," or the sound of the event as it is happening; 2) voice reports in which newsmen describe the event and 3) interviews with important figures and those involved in news stories. There is another possibility when it comes to those events of overriding importance that require elaborate special coverage, such as elections, space adventures and the like. Often such events occupy long hours of air time with one or two anchor men knitting together the reports of correspondents at various pickups or "remote" locations in which it is expected that news will be made. Telephone lines enable newsmen to broadcast "live" where major events are taking place. But these are the extraordinary events. Much more commonly, the reporter or correspondent is armed with his tape recorder and sent off to the scene of an anticipated story to develop the best coverage his experience and imagination allow. It should be pointed out here, also, that in joint radio-television news operations, it is common for the reporter to handle coverage for both media. This is accomplished by having the correspondent operate two microphones, one for a tape recorder and the other for a sound camera, as he delivers his report or conducts interviews. It also is possible to make a "dub," or duplicate tape recording, from the film sound track after the film has been returned to news headquarters and while it is being screened.

When the radio correspondent covers a story within range of home base, his problems usually are small. He checks out the basic advance information, covers the story, and returns with his tapes and story notes to construct a package that he feels tells his story more than just adequately. When the reporter goes out of town, he may have to feed his report and actuality tape back to his home office, either on the telephone or on a leased audio line. It is possible in certain situations for the reporter to ship his tapes back by plane, train, bus or courier, depending on the story and the time element. On breaking news, it is more common to feed it back as soon as possible for use as soon as it can be put on the air. When a network correspondent is sent somewhere to cover a story, arrangements usually are made for him to go to the nearest affiliated station to feed from there. Sometimes the network news headquarters simply will ask a newsman at that affiliate to cover the story, depending on the magnitude of the event, network requirements and the network's faith in the judgment of the affiliate's reporters. Most radio stations are geared to receive network programming but not to originate such material.

When arrangements are made to feed from an affiliate to the network, it must be ascertained whether or not an audio telephone "loop" is available. If not, one must be ordered—in

Bank of 9 audio tape cartridge playback machines.
(Courtesy Norman Goldman)

advance—so that the report can be sent. Typical audio line charges in the U.S. run to about 15c per mile. Reports also can be fed from overseas at correspondingly higher costs. World capitals and important cities can be "ordered up" on short notice, usually less than an hour. Typical charges run to about $4 per minute, with a minimum order of ten minutes required. The communications satellites also provide audio service, but at a cost of something like three times more than regular overseas service. As a point of interest, it might also be noted that sometimes grave and often forbidding complications arise when special news coverage is desired in such far off places as India, for instance. The British Post Office still controls communications with the sub-continent, and it requires 24 hours notice to order broadcasting facilities from New Delhi. This, of course, is a great deterrent to such coverage.

In network operations, it is not uncommon for experienced correspondents to be given authority to order line facilities for stories they know their home office will want as quickly as possible. They would make such arrangements wherever they are—in London, Paris, Rome, Saigon, or wherever, then send a cable to or telephone New York saying that they will be up on a circuit at a specified time. It is also common practice for foreign correspondents to feed more than one spot when a circuit has been ordered. This saves the time and expense of reordering and meeting separate circuits.

Whether the reporter is covering a local, national or international story, there are certain things he should do as a matter of course to expedite the use of his material. If he is any distance from his office, he should telephone as soon as he has his story to tell his editor what and how much he has and when he thinks it will be ready for the air. Perhaps he needs some time to write his story, including cues to various interviews and elements within that report. He might also have some suggestions on how the introduction to his spot should be written. Then, the experienced radio or television reporter usually casts his story in such a way that the introduction and the report, will mesh cleanly. Greatly to be shunned, both in radio and television news, is the so-called "echo lead-in," which, as the name implies, is that awkward situation in which an introduction uses words that duplicate the wordage of the taped report. This can be avoided by carefully listening to the tape before writing the intro. Even in those last-minute situations in which there's a great rush to make the air, every effort should be made to "monitor" or listen to the tape to avoid that over-lapping verbiage. This is a point that is repeated throughout this text because it is a keystone to smooth, well-sounding newscasts, both on radio and television.

Lead-ins to tape and film reports usually are brief, only a matter of ten or 15 seconds. It shouldn't take much effort, then, for the person writing the intro to check the spot and find something informative that is not in the report and use it to get into the story. If it will be a late feed, the writer often can talk to the correspondent and come to some kind of agreement on a way of setting up the spot properly. For instance, if the field reporter is covering an accident, he and the writer might agree that the reporter will not touch on the statistics but instead will dwell on the circumstances of the event. In this way, the intro writer can report that, say, seven people were hurt today when two cars were involved in a crash at such-and-such a place. Then, with just the additional line that so-and-so has the story, the tape is properly cued and smoothly on air. This practice pertains, of course, only in situations in which the voice report is about to be taped or fed and the writer and reporter can in fact take time to consult. On the other hand, when the field reporter is taping and shipping his report and the opportunity to consult does not exist, the reporter can aid his own cause and that of the intro writer by leaving something for the intro writer to say. For instance, in taping a report on a congressional action or a vote by a state legislature or city council, the reporter might simply say what the actual vote count was in such a way that he will pick right up from the obvious information that the lead-in will convey. An example would be something like this:

> ANCHORMAN: THE U.S. SENATE MADE AN IM-
> PORTANT DECISION TODAY. IT KILLED A CON-
> TROVERSIAL PROJECT THAT WOULD HAVE COM-
> MITTED THE UNITED STATES TO A LONG-RANGE
> EXPLORATION OF DEEP SPACE. MORE ON THAT
> NOW FROM TOBY ESTEVEZ:

> ESTEVEZ: THE VOTE WAS FIFTY-ONE TO FORTY-
> NINE. CLOSE, AS EXPECTED, BUT A BIG DISAP-
> POINTMENT FOR THE WHITE HOUSE. THE
> PRESIDENT HAD INSISTED THAT THE COUNTRY'S
> PRESTIGE WAS AT STAKE IN THE PROGRAM TO
> SEND A SPACE SHIP TO MARS.

The report probably would continue for another half-minute or so to round out the details.

The point is that there normally is more interesting information about any news story than the radio or television newsman can possibly cover. With just a bit of effort, the introduction to a field report can and should be made a useful adjunct to the story, setting it up properly so the listener or viewer is prepared for what he is about to see or hear. Similarly, it sometimes is necessary to round out a report with additional important information that has been developed since the report was filed. There are many situations on fast-breaking news stories or just routine events when the flow of either is so swift as to outdate a report filed sometimes only minutes but more often hours before a newscast. Then, there is no alternative than to junk the spot and have the anchorman tell the story on the basis of the latest information.

Six mornings every week, all these problems of domestic and international news coverage are handled smoothly and efficiently in the format of the CBS World News Roundup. It is the chief outlet of CBS Radio News for information on world events that have occurred while most Americans slept. It is important to remember that when it is midnight in the U.S., it is mid-day in Asia and dawn is near in Europe. Throughout the night, the CBS Radio News team in New York is gearing up for the Roundup. Producer Hal Terkel is on hand all night long, checking the wires and cables from correspondents and laying out the Roundup for that morning. Correspondent Dallas Townsend is at his desk long hours before most Americans begin to awaken. Then, at 8 AM in New York, Mondays through Saturdays, Townsend takes the air with this prestige production of CBS Radio News. The following is the transcript of the World News Roundup broadcast on Monday, November 30, 1970. It was a rather routine news day but perhaps just a bit livelier than Mondays usually are after weekends in which business and commerce throughout most of the world have had a 2-day hiatus. Townsend writes all his own broadcast material and begins the day for millions of Americans with a clear, crisp, authoritative look at the changing world:

TOWNSEND: Israel again accuses Egypt of violating Suez Canal cease-fire.

New air incident over North Viet Nam.

Pope arrives in Australia.

Washington watches dispute over Lithuanian sailor.

Egeberg reported on the way out.

Israel this morning once again accused Egypt of violating the cease-fire in the Suez Canal zone. Larry Pomeroy has the story in Tel Aviv:

POMEROY: ISRAEL CLAIMS THAT CONSTRUCTION WORK HAS STARTED ON NEW SITES FOR ANTI-AIRCRAFT MISSILES IN THE EGYPTIAN HALF OF THE SUEZ CANAL ZONE. A MILITARY SPOKESMAN SAID A COMPLAINT OUTLINING THIS LATEST VIOLATION OF THE CEASE-FIRE HAS BEEN SUBMITTED TO THE UNITED NATIONS. IT WOULD BE ISRAEL'S 26th CHARGE THAT EGYPT HAS BROKEN THE TERMS OF THE STANDSTILL TRUCE. MEANWHILE, ISRAEL'S AMBASSADOR TO WASHINGTON, YITZAK RABIN, IS NOW ON HIS WAY BACK TO THE UNITED STATES CAPITAL AFTER A BRIEF VISIT HERE. IT'S UNDERSTOOD THAT

DEFENSE MINISTER DAYAN WILL JOIN HIM IN WASHINGTON IN A WEEK'S TIME FOR TOP LEVEL TALKS WITH MEMBERS OF THE NIXON ADMINISTRATION, INCLUDING, PERHAPS, THE PRESIDENT, HIMSELF. THE OUTCOME OF THOSE MEETINGS IS EXPECTED TO DETERMINE HOW SOON ISRAEL RETURNS TO THE SUSPENDED MIDDLE EAST PEACE TALKS.

LARRY POMEROY, CBS NEWS, TEL AVIV.

TOWNSEND: In Southeast Asis, the Viet Cong today said it will observe a three-day truce at both Christmas and New Years, and a four-day truce during the lunar New Year in late January.

Saigon today is talking about a new air incident north of the buffer zone. We'll hear about it from Gary Shepard:

SHEPARD: FOR THE SECOND TIME IN LESS THAN TWO WEEKS, AN AMERICAN COMBAT AIRCRAFT HAS HIT A COMMUNIST TARGET INSIDE NORTH VIET NAM. THE US MILITARY COMMAND REPORTED TODAY THAT THE LATEST AIR RAID INVOLVED AN F-105 FIGHTER BOMBER WHICH HIT A RADAR CONTROLLED ANTI-AIRCRAFT BATTERY FIVE-AND-A-HALF MILES NORTH OF THE DEMILITARIZED ZONE, ONLY A SHORT DISTANCE FROM THE BORDER WITH LAOS. THE OFFICIAL COMMUNIQUE SAYS THE RAID AMOUNTED TO PROTECTIVE REACTION WHICH IS DEFINED AS THE INHERENT RIGHT OF SELF-DEFENSE. A MILITARY SPOKESMAN SAID LATER THE ATTACK WAS IN RESPONSE TO AN OVERT HOSTILE ACTION BY THE ENEMY. RELIABLE MILITARY SOURCES HAD ADDITIONAL DETAILS: TWO F-105S WERE HITTING COMMUNIST TARGETS ALONG THE HO CHI MINH TRAIL IN LAOS, THEY SAY, WHEN THEY RECEIVED ANTI-AIRCRAFT FIRE FROM THE COMMUNIST BATTERY ACROSS THE BORDER INSIDE NORTH VIET NAM. THE PILOT OF ONE OF THE PLANES DECIDED THAT IF HE DIDN'T ATTACK THE ANTI-AIRCRAFT SITE HE PROBABLY WOULD BE SHOT DOWN. AS A RESULT, HE FLEW ACROSS THE BORDER, BOMBED THE INSTALLATION AND WITH THE SECOND PLANE RETURNED TO HIS BASE. THERE IS NO REPORT WHETHER THE GUN SITE

WAS DAMAGED OR DESTROYED.
GARY SHEPARD, CBS NEWS, SAIGON.

TOWNSEND: The U.S. Command, in its official report on this episode, does not say that the North Viet Namese anti-aircraft battery actually opened fire. It does say that the F-105 picked up electronic indications that the battery was getting a fix on some B-52S that the fighter-bomber was escorting. CBS News Correspondent Bob Schieffer reports that officials at the Pentagon say this latest incident should come as no surprise to the North Viet Namese. They say the newly-defined policy of protective reaction was clearly outlined last week at the Pentagon. And in a new clarification of that policy, a Pentagon spokesman says that—once the ground gunner locks in with his Radar—the pilot is free to attack. He does not have to wait until he is actually fired on.

The combination of the Shepard report and the "tag" Townsend put on it demonstrate some of the difficulties in the short and long-range reporting of a war in which official communiques often omit more information than they give out. Shepard had to quote "reliable military sources" on what supposedly happened. In his "come out," or tag, Townsend points out the discrepancy between the official version and what the "sources" were saying, and he goes on to quote another CBS News Correspondent who covers the Department of Defense in an effort to clarify some confusing information about the U.S. role in the war. This treatment by Townsend shows how the newscaster must be constantly alert for ways to tie diffuse elements of a story together.

TOWNSEND: Communist party and government leaders of Soviet Russia and the East European communist countries will hold a summit conference in East Berlin later this week. That was announced this morning by Moscow. The belief is that they will try to agree on a unified approach to West Germany's eastern policy, including its news accords with Soviet Russia and Poland...and pending West German negotiations with Czechoslovakia.

Leonid Brezhnev had some optimistic comments over the weekend on the chances for settling the Berlin problem. But the Soviet Communist party leader made it clear that Soviet Russia will not overlook the interests of

CBS Morning Report anchorman Dallas Townsend. (Courtesy Norman Goldman)

East Germany, which surrounds Berlin. Brezhnev spoke in Armenia, during ceremonies marking the fiftieth anniversary of that Soviet Republic. Observers in Moscow view his remarks as a sign that Moscow would be most unlikely to sacrifice East German interests for the sake of a Berlin solution. Brezhnev used the occasion for another strong attack on United States' involvement in Southeast Asia...specifically the recent attempt to rescue American prisoners of war in North Viet Nam, and the bombing raids over that country. Brezhnev criticized what he called "the brazen attempt by some United States officials to legalize such banditry...giving the United States the right, so to speak, to behave as unrestricted masters of the territory and air space of other countries." As for conditions in Europe, Brezhnev said the political climate there has improved, and there are noticeable chances for better relations.

Pope Paul arrived in Australia a few hours ago...after a brief stop in American Samoa and the newly-independent nation of Western Samoa. Strict security was in force because of last week's attempt against his life in the Philippines but Harold Abrahams reports that the Pontiff received a warm welcome in Sydney:

ABRAHAMS: THE POPE'S VISIT TO AUSTRALIA GOT OFF TO A VERY GOOD START. HIS WARMTH AND FRIENDSHIP IS APPARENT TO EVERYONE WHO'S SEEN HIM. RIGHT FROM THE TIME HE ARRIVED AT SYDNEY AIRPORT HE SET THE TENOR OF THE VISIT. HAVING DISPOSED OF THE OFFICIAL SPEECH BY PRIME MINISTER GORDON, IT WAS ONLY A FEW MINUTES BEFORE HE BROKE FROM THE PREPARED PROGRAM TO PLUNGE INTO THE CROWD, ALTERNATELY HOLDING HANDS WITH PEOPLE AND RAISING HIS HANDS IN BLESSING. AT TIMES, HE WAS SUBMERGED IN THE CROWD...ALL THAT COULD BE SEEN OF HIM WAS THE TOP OF HIS HEAD AND OCCASIONALLY AN UPRAISED HAND. CLOSE AT HAND AT ALL TIMES WAS THE HUGE FRAME OF BISHOP MAR-SINKAS...THE MAN WHO'S THE POPE'S BODYGUARD AND HIS OFFICIAL ENVOY IN PLANNING THE ENTIRE 29,000 MILE TOUR. THE CROWD, WHILE ENTHUSIASTIC, WAS RESTRAINED AND AT NO TIME WAS THE MUCH-PUBLICIZED SECURITY SYSTEM REQUIRED TO TAKE ANY AC-TION. IF THE REST OF THE SYDNEY VISIT FOLLOWS THIS COURSE, NONE OF THE FEARS WILL BE REALIZED.

HAROLD ABRAHAMS IN SYDNEY, AUSTRALIA.

Notice here the way Abrahams signs off his report. He is a "stringer," or Part-Time reporter, and therefore cannot use the CBS News designation.

Notice, also, the natural bridge that picks up from the Abrahams spot to the next audio insert.

TOWNSEND: Ordinarily, the Pope's long journey would be getting top coverage today in Rome, but Frank Kearns reports that principal attention is focused instead on what's going on in the Italian Parliament:

KEARNS: POPE PAUL'S VISIT TO THE FAR EAST HAS ALREADY TAKEN SECOND PLACE IN THE NEWS HERE. INSTEAD, ALL ATTENTION IS FOCUSED ON THE CHAMBER OF DEPUTIES WHERE ANY HOUR NOW SLEEPY DEPUTIES ARE EXPECTED TO CAST THEIR FINAL VOTE ON THE BILL TO GIVE ITALIANS A DIVORCE LAW FOR THE FIRST TIME IN MORE THAN A CENTURY. MOST INNER CIRCLES EXPECT THE BILL TO PASS, PERHAPS BY A SLIM MAJORITY BUT ITS SO CONTROVERSIAL AND HISTORIC THAT EVEN TOP SOURCES ADMIT THE OUTCOME IS LITERALLY UNPREDICTABLE. DEPUTIES HAVE BEEN MEETING NON-STOP SINCE LAST TUESDAY ON THIS AND A VITAL TAX BILL. PRIME MINISTER AMELIO COLOMBO'S GOVERNMENT OVER THE WEEKEND WON A VOTE OF CONFIDENCE ON AN AMENDMENT TO THE TAX BILL, BUT DEFINITIVE VOTING ON THAT MEASURE HAS BEEN POSTPONED UNTIL THE FINAL BALLOTING ON THE DIVORCE BILL. A VOTE IS EXPECTED LATER TODAY OR TONIGHT.
FRANK KEARNS, CBS NEWS, ROME.

TOWNSEND: West Germany's Ambassador to Portugal, Hans Schmidt-Yoricks, aged 61, and his wife, 56, committed suicide last night in Lisbon. The West German Embassy there says they killed themselves for personal reasons, and does not elaborate.

A storm is blowing up in Washington over what happened a week ago in international waters off Martha's Vineyard, Massachusetts. A Lithuanian sailor tried to defect from a Soviet fishing vessel...jumping onto the deck of a Coast Guard cutter...but the cutter allowed Soviet sailors to come aboard, beat up the Lithuanian and drag him back to their own ship. CBS News Diplomatic Correspondent Marvin Kalb reports the conflicting explanations of how this was allowed to happen:

KALB: THE COAST GUARD IS TRYING TO PLACE THE BLAME ON THE STATE DEPARTMENT AND

THE STATE DEPARTMENT INSISTS THERE IS NO QUESTION THE BLAME BELONGS ON THE COAST GUARD. FOGGY BOTTOM OFFICIALS FAMILIAR WITH ALL OF THE DETAILS MAINTAIN THAT COAST GUARD HEADQUARTERS IN BOSTON CONTACTED THE STATE DEPARTMENT BEFORE THE SOVIET SEAMAN ACTUALLY JUMPED ONTO THE AMERICAN SHIP, WHEN THERE WAS ONLY AN INDICATION A DEFECTION MIGHT TAKE PLACE, NOT THE FACT THAT IT DID. AT THAT TIME, THE STATE DEPARTMENT SAID THE UNITED STATES DID NOT WANT TO PROVOKE A DEFECTION, BUT THE STATE DEPARTMENT OFFICIAL WHO SAID THIS WAS NO MORE PRECISE. THE COAST GUARD READ HIS IMPRESSION AS MEANING: DON'T ALLOW THE DEFECTION TO TAKE PLACE. FOR THAT REASON, IT IS SAID, WHEN THE SEAMAN JUMPED AND REMAINED IN AMERICAN HANDS FOR FIVE HOURS, THE COST GUARD ALLOWED THE RUSSIANS TO BOARD THE AMERICAN SHIP, BEAT THE SOVIET CITIZEN INTO UNCONSCIOUSNESS AND TAKE HIM BACK TO THE RUSSIAN SHIP. DEPARTMENT OFFICIALS SAY IT IS UNBELIEVABLE THAT THE COAST GUARD COULD HAVE ALLOWED THAT TO HAPPEN. THEY NOW FEAR CONGRESS WILL MAKE AN ISSUE OF IT, EMBARRASS THE ADMINISTRATION AND, THESE OFFICIALS ADD, THERE IS NOTHING THEY CAN NOW DO TO HELP EITHER THE SOVIET SEAMAN OR THE AD MINISTRATION.

MARVIN KALB, CBS NEWS, WASHINGTON.

TOWNSEND: Demonstrations protesting the incident off Martha's Vineyard were staged over the weekend by Lithuanian, Latvian and Estonian groups in several large American cities. Here in New York, the Lithuanian-American action committee says President Nixon should declare in public that the denial of asylum to the Lithuanian sailor was a mistake on the part of some United States officials. Otherwise, this group says, people behind the Iron Curtain will lose faith in the United States.

Sometime this week, perhaps today, the White House plans to issue its second so-called "inflation alert"...and it's expected to be much stronger than the first one, which was released during the summer. That one merely listed product areas which had experienced relatively rapid price increases at the wholesale level. The new inflation alert, almost certainly, will pinpoint specific unions and industries. The probable targets of such criticism will be the Teamsters Union and the trucking industry, the United Auto Workers and the auto makers, the oil industry and the construction workers' union. All of these unions and industries have been parties to above average increases in wage costs and prices to the consumer in recent months. Washington sources say the inflation alert will urge corporations not to react to new wage settlements by passing on extra costs to consumers...which is what General Motors did in announcing higher prices for its new cars. However, President Nixon is not expected to apply direct pressure or persuasion...or to establish voluntary wage-price guidelines...a move tried by both the Kennedy and Johnson Administrations.

Five days ago, President Nixon fired Walter Hickel as Secretary of the Interior...and now, according to CBS News Washington Correspondent Daniel Schorr, the ax is about to swing again:

SCHORR: THE NIXON ADMINISTRATION IS PREPARING TO UNSEAT ANOTHER HIGH OFFICIAL, DOCTOR ROGER EGEBERG, ITS TOP HEALTH OFFICER. DOCTOR EGEBERG, FORMER MEDICAL SCHOOL DEAN AT THE UNIVERSITY OF SOUTHERN CALIFORNIA, WAS HASTILY NAMED ASSISTANT SECRETARY AT THE DEPARTMENT OF HEALTH, EDUCATION AND WELFARE A LITTLE LESS THAN A YEAR-AND-A-HALF AGO, AFTER THE APPOINTMENT OF DOCTOR JOHN KNOWLES OF BOSTON WAS KILLED AS A RESULT OF CONSERVATIVE OPPOSITION. DOCTOR EGEBERG HAS NOT ENDEARED HIMSELF AT THE WHITE HOUSE AND HAS CAUSED ADDITIONAL IRRITATION BY HIS PENCHANT FOR TALKING OPENLY ABOUT HIS DIFFICULTY OF GETTING THROUGH TO THE PRESIDENT ABOUT PRESSING HEALTH PROBLEMS. LIKE WALTER HICKEL, HE'S HOLDING OUT FOR AN "ARROW-IN-THE-HEART" FIRING AND PLANS FOR THAT ARE ADVANCED ENOUGH FOR INTERVIEWS TO BE IN PROGRESS WITH POSSIBLE SUCCESSORS. THE CANDIDATE OF THE NEW ESTABLISHMENT IS UNDERSTOOD TO BE DOCTOR

CHARLES EDWARDS, FOOD AND DRUG COM-
MISSIONER. ANOTHER CANDIDATE, IS DOCTOR
NEAL SOLOMON, SECRETARY OF HEALTH FOR THE
STATE OF MARYLAND, A FRIEND OF VICE
PRESIDENT AGNEW, WHO AT ONE TIME TREATED
MRS. AGNEW. DOCTOR EGEBERG, RECENTLY
BACK FROM A TOUR OF THE SOVIET UNION, IS
EXPECTED ONE WAY OR THE OTHER TO GET THE
WORD SOON THAT HE IS OUT.
DANIEL SCHORR, CBS NEWS, WASHINGTON.

TOWNSEND: The Washington Star and the New York
Times this morning say one of ousted Secretary Hickel's
chief aides...dismissed on Friday...has refused to submit
his resignation. They say Doctor Leslie Glasgow,
Assistant Secretary for Fish, Wildlife, Parks and Marine
Resources, plans to be at his desk today, Glasglow is
described as incredulous at his firing.

Treasury Secretary David Kennedy, who has been
rumored on his way out, said today in Rome that
President Nixon has not asked for his resignation and he
has not offered it. Kennedy made that statement in reply
to questions about the stories circulating in Washington.

Senator Abraham Ribicoff plans to introduce new
legislation today in the Senate aimed at getting the federal
government to support school and neighborhood integration throughout the country. The Connecticut
Democrat, a former Secretary of Health, Education and
Welfare, says the legislation includes economic incentives
to encourage and help local communities and states to
promote integration in schools and housing. CBS
Newsman Tony Sargent, reporting from Washington, says
Ribicoff feels that a school integration program must
include efforts to break down segregated housing patterns
to avoid failure in major metropolitan areas. With that in
mind, one of his proposed measures would allow only one
school district for each metropolitan area, no matter how
large that area might be. An arrangement of this type,
Ribicoff thinks, would ensure that all schools involved
could be brought more nearly into racial balance.
Students could be sent to any school in the area, regardless of city, county or even state lines. Another Ribicoff
bill would place the federal government behind moves to
find housing for minority groups in suburbs.

The long-distance runners are getting ready to run again...but not right now. Over the weekend, Joel Ahlstrom, aged 29, and his brother, Tony, aged 22, completed a 270-mile run from Chicago to Detroit...their purpose being to call attention to the campaign against pollution. They averaged 27 miles a day...running through rain, snow and cold weather...stopping in ten cities to pass out anti-pollution literature. And it turns out that this was only a warm-up for the much more elaborate jaunt they plan for next summer. In that one, the Ahlstrom brothers plan to run 2,000 miles...all the way from California to New York...to raise money for a new chapel at their college in Illinois.

Dallas Townsend, CBS News.

TAPED INSERT FAILURE

After the script has been finished, a newscaster must not overlook another important area before he can go on the air. For his own professional protection, he must make certain he can cover in the event of any technical failure with an audio tape. To do so, he usually provides himself with some kind of standby material. It is pretty much standard practice in network operations to prepare verbatim transcripts of taped spots from which the newscasters and writers work in preparing lead-ins and lead-outs. This practice simplifies matters when it comes to standby material because the newscaster can insert a copy of that transcript at the proper place in his script. Then, if the audio tape should not come up as planned, the newscaster can politely excuse the failure away and report as much of the spot from the transcript as he feels is needed to do the story justice. By the same token, he could pick up in the transcript if the tape should break on the air, an infrequent occurrence, but something that does happen from time to time. For the newsman who doesn't have the luxury of verbatim transcripts, it is essential to make detailed notes of the contents of taped spots that he will write into or out of so that those notes can serve as standby copy when he takes air. In those cases where someone else monitors and writes into and out of a spot, the newscaster should insist that the writer provide him with a synopsis of the spot for standby copy.

NEWS FEATURES

Beyond the normal daily flow of "hard" news on the air, there is a little-tapped reservoir of "sidebar" and human interest material that so often can add a bright, new dimension in the effort to keep a community or a nation informed. It is unfortunate that time requirements so often force this material to be shoved aside. The unhappy truth is that the regular budget of disaster, crisis and turmoil is so appallingly extensive that it eats up most of the air time available for news. This is especially true of radio stations that conform to the pattern of frequent, short newscasts, and the complaint holds true, also, in television news, where pictorial content so often is confined to statements from public figures and those involved in the day-to-day effort to make local, state and national governments function and the stories that illustrate the horde of man-made problems at home and abroad. Unfortunately, news usually wears a somber face, but it is ridiculous to decree that any fixed part of daily radio or television news output must be set aside for a sampling of the "good" news that can be found when someone takes the trouble to look for it.

Newspapers always have had and still do have the advantage of being able to background a story. When a good newspaper decided to do a "take-out" on a news story or a news feature, it often will devote not just columns but entire pages to that effort. If someone were to read those enterprise pieces aloud they would take up great amounts of time that broadcasters only infrequently are willing to devote to any news or news related item. When a major calamity occurs, of course, normal programming is abandoned and all attention centered on that event, but that ordinarily requires an event of transcendental importance such as the death of a president. Lesser but still extra-ordinarily important events often produce extra air time for special coverage, but in the day-to-day coverage of the news, much that is interesting in its own right simply is discarded. Then, too, many newsmen and women take themselves so terribly seriously that they ignore those stories that can be just plain fun. Because the 15-minute radio newscast is so rare anymore, the old device of rounding off a newscast with a "kicker" or light story is employed less and less frequently. It is true that genuine humor is rare and those with an unerring instinct for it even rarer. With the expansion of radio and television news, however, there may be increasing opportunities for newsmen to experiment with deeper backgrounding of stories for greater understanding, for more frequent use of sidebar material that conveys greater detail and, ultimately, perhaps even a greater effort to poke a bit of fun at ourselves or at least to break up the often dismal character of so much of the news.

CBS anchorman and feature writer, **Charles Osgood**.

There are newsmen who have that almost magical touch that permits them to see into and through human beings and conditions and thereby bring out unexpected, revealing and entertaining aspects of news or feature stories. One of these responsible and imaginative reporters is Charles Osgood of radio station WCBS. In addition to his regular morning anchor assignment on that all-news station, Osgood writes, produces and broadcasts a daily feature on the CBS Radio Network. It is called "Profiles." From the spur of a way-out wire service story, a newspaper item or perhaps by letting his own imagination play over an event gaining public attention, Osgood always comes up with interesting material. Frequently, he will tape an interview on the telephone with the central character of his report, edit it in a highly-imaginative way and thereby bring out sometimes surprising and always interesting aspects of his report. At other times, he just tells it the way he sees it, or thinks an event should have happened. A typical example of the Osgood flair and style follows. In it, he combines a sports phenomenom with a theme that has been dealt with in literature and musical comedy and puts his own, wonderful twist on the story:

I HAPPEN TO KNOW GEORGE BLANDA'S SECRET...AND I WILL LET YOU IN ON IT IN JUST A MOMENT: (COMMERCIAL)

ONE NIGHT ABOUT SIX WEEKS AGO, AN AGING PRO FOOTBALL SUBSTITUTE QUARTERBACK AND EXTRA POINT KICKER SAT IN HIS STUDY, RUBBING LINAMENT INTO HIS ACHING LIMBS...WHEN SUDDENLY THERE WAS A PUFF OF SMOKE...A FIENDISH LAUGH...AND THERE STOOD A STRANGE LOOKING FELLOW WITH CLOVEN HOOVES...A PITCHFORK...AND A PROPOSITION. "BLANDA," HE SAID, "HOW WOULD YOU LIKE TO BE THE TALK OF THE NATION...THE BIGGEST FOOTBALL HERO OF ALL?"

(BLANDA) "I AM 43...SIX YEARS OLDER THAN MY COACH. I ONLY KICK EXTRA POINTS AND OCCASIONAL FIELD GOALS AND SO STOP PUTTING ME ON AND GET OUT OF HERE."

BUT, BEFORE HE DISAPPEARED IN HIS PUFF OF SMOKE, THE VISITOR LAUGHED ANOTHER FIENDISH LAUGH AND SAID: "WAIT 'TILL YOU SEE WHAT HAPPENS SUNDAY!"

THAT SUNDAY...STAR QUARTERBACK DARYL LAMONICA SPRAINED HIS BACK. BLANDA WAS SENT IN AND THREW TWO TOUCHDOWN PASSES...AND CONVERTED THE EXTRA POINTS..AS OAKLAND BEAT PITTSBURGH, 31 TO 14.

ONE NIGHT THAT WEEK, BLANDA WAS ALONE IN HIS STUDY WHEN AGAIN CAME THE PUFF OF

SMOKE AND THE FIENDISH LAUGH...AND THE
FELLOW WITH THE PITCHFORK AND THE CLOVEN
HOOVES WAS SAYING: "HOW DID YOU LIKE THEM
APPLES?"

"GET OUT OF HERE," SAID BLANDA. IF I
THOUGHT YOU SPRAINED LAMONICA'S BACK I'D
KICK YOU THROUGH THE UPRIGHTS."

BUT, THE FELLOW JUST LAUGHED AGAIN.

NEXT SUNDAY; WITH JUST SECONDS LEFT IN
THE GAME, GEORGE BLANDA KICKED A 48-YARD
FIELD GOAL...AND OAKLAND TIED THE WORLD
CHAMPION KANSAS CITY CHIEFS. 17 TO 17.

NOW, BLANDA WAS AFRAID TO GO INTO HIS
STUDY ANYMORE. BUT HE DID...AND SURE
ENOUGH THERE WAS THE PUFF OF SMOKE...AND
HIS OLD FIENDISH FRIEND. "WHAT DO YOU WANT?
WHY ARE YOU DOING THIS?" SAID BLANDA.
"NEVER MIND," SAID THE FIERY VISITOR. "I WILL
TELL YOU SOON ENOUGH. FOR NOW, JUST WAIT
'TILL THIS SUNDAY"...AND HE WAS GONE.

THAT SUNDAY, BLANDA CAME IN FOR
LAMONICA AGAIN...THREW A TOUCHDOWN PASS TO
WARREN WELLS...AND TIED THE GAME WITH
CLEVELAND WITH 89 SECONDS LEFT TO PLAY. THE
FANS WENT WILD. THEN, WITH THREE SECONDS IN
THE GAME...THE OLD MAN ATTEMPTED A FIELD
GOAL FROM HIS OWN 48-YARD LINE...A 52-YARD
ATTEMPT. THE BALL CAME UP OFF HIS TOE...AND
AS IF IT HAD A PAIR OF WINGS AND EYES...FLEW
RIGHT THROUGH THE UPRIGHTS AND OVER THE
CROSSBAR. OAKLAND WON, 23 TO 20.

NOW, BLANDA KNEW. NEXT TIME HE'D FIND
OUT WHAT WAS WANTED OF HIM. THAT WEEK...-
WHEN THE PUFF OF SMOKE CAME...HE FOUND
OUT ALL RIGHT. BUT WOULD HE DO IT? COULD HE
PAY THAT HIGH A PRICE? HE SAID HE WOULD
THINK ABOUT IT. "GOOD," SAID THE VISITOR.
MEANWHILE I'LL BE WITH YOU SUNDAY.

THAT SUNDAY, THE RAIDERS WERE LOSING TO
DENVER...'TILL THEY BROUGHT BLANDA IN AND
BLANDA THREW THREE LONG PASSES..THE LAST
FOR A TOUCHDOWN...AND OAKLAND WON, 24 TO 19.

AND, YES...YESTERDAY...WITH SEVEN
SECONDS LEFT IN THE GAME WITH SAN
DIEGO...THEY CALLED ON GEORGE BLANDA...AND

HE KICKED ANOTHER FIELD GOAL...AND OAKLAND WON, 20 TO 17.

GEORGE BLANDA SEEMS THE SAME AS BEFORE...BUT FRIENDS WONDER WHY HE'S SPENDING SO MUCH TIME ALONE IN HIS STUDY THESE FALL NIGHTS...WHY THE FIENDISH LAUGHTER SEEMS TO BE GETTING LOUDER.

CAN THERE BE ANY DOUBT?

IT IS THE DEVIL'S WORK...AND WHAT THE DEVIL WANTS IS NOT JUST ANOTHER SOUL...HE'S GOT PLENTY OF THEM.

WHAT HE WANTS IS TWO TICKETS TO THE SUPERBOWL!

AND NOW THIS MESSAGE: (COMMERCIAL)

THIS IS CHARLES OSGOOD, WITH "PROFILE" ON CBS RADIO.

CHAPTER 7

Television News

Journalism approaches its highest potential of effectiveness in television news, with its ability to capture the major happenings of our time and deliver sound and visual reports to the homes of viewers. The fulfillment of this ideal remains somewhere in the distance, but the increasing amount of time, effort and money invested in television news indicates progress. The impact of the medium is perhaps best demonstrated by the numbers who rely exclusively on television for news.

In fairness, however, it is doubtful that even the most ardent advocate of broadcast journalism would claim that an information diet made up only of television news would sustain an informed citizen. Indeed, the greatest frustration of those working in television news is the realization of how really little information can be conveyed in the still limited time available. This problem remains, although substantial progress has been noted in recent years. A study made for the Radio and Television News Directors Association showed that in 1960 television stations were putting on an average of just over four hours of news each week. In the beginning of 1970, that figure had risen to an average of just over nine hours a week. The era of the 15-minute newscast largely had given way to the half-hour format which, obviously, doubled the potential for getting information on the air.

Beyond that, and perhaps even more indicative of the growing importance of news, was the vastly increased amount of money that commercial television stations were putting into their coverage. According to the RTNDA study, news budgets for TV stations in the top 50 markets rose from an average of $121,000 in 1960 to $440,000 in 1970. Out of a total of 174 stations queried, 123 responded. They reported they were spending more than a combined total of $51,505,000 for news in 1970, compared to $10,670,000 in 1960. Another significant finding of the RTNDA study was that stations had recognized the importance of trained personnel in preparing and presenting news that is both respectable and salable. Total staffs of the stations surveyed numbered 747 in 1960 and 2,990 in 1970.

As more time, effort, manpower and money were invested in television news, another interesting phenomenon became apparent, at least to the management of local television stations. Suddenly, their "loss leader" was becoming a profit maker. The old axiom that the news department was a necessary, money-losing evil was shown to be false. In the areas of head-on competition, station A was finding it was being pressed by station B in the area of news coverage as news audiences increased and advertisers looked more and more to news as the place to spend their money. Suddenly, news directors were walking around the studios with their heads up, with the feeling of being a contributing part of the organization. No longer was it necessary to go to management with hat in hand when they needed something to improve their product or had to make a pitch for extra air time.

In a major study of local television news, **Broadcasting Magazine** noted early in 1970 that only the smallest station it looked into was still showing red ink on its news operation and even the manager of that station said he considered his investment in news to be well worth the cost.

Still another radical sort of shift in viewpoint on television and television news is worth noting here. In its first broad look at the field of broadcast journalism in 1968, the panel of jurors deciding the Alfred I. duPont-Columbia University awards were less than complimentary. In part, at least, their report pictured broadcasters as money-grubbing suppliers of shallow programming. A year later, however, in their "Survey of Broadcast Journalism 1969-70: Year of Challenge, Year of Crisis," the panel came out with quite a different view. The report declared: "It seemed to us that this year many stories were more deeply humane, told by men increasingly able and willing to penetrate the subtleties of life in America in the last half of the 20th century. Reporting skills and resources had grown impressively, particularly on the local level. Although frequently the picture presented was appalling, the courage of broadcasters in showing it to us lifted our spirits in some mysterious way. For in the process of exposing suffering and degregation, violence and stupidity, the man who wrote, filmed and broadcast these programs seemed to be saying that something must and can be done, that Americans still are capable of improvement and correction. At its most devastating, broadcast journalism was at its most helpful."

NETWORK AND LOCAL NEWS COVERAGE

In television, as in radio, it is essential to take notice of the distinction between network and local, or independent, news

91

operations. Here, again, the major networks are committed to and consumed by the task of providing broad coverage of the entire world, the kind of news coverage that simply is beyond the resources of independent stations no matter how zealous they may be. This is not to imply that independent stations are locked out when it comes to national and international affairs. They have the opportunity to subscribe to various syndicated news services and thus put together their own blend of local, national and international news. Beyond that, there are hundreds of individuals and companies with multiple station holdings that are arranged into smaller networks that are geared to meet the interests and needs of their owners and viewers. Each one of these must make the corporate decision as to the commitment it will make to news and how best to discharge that responsibility.

It should be noted here, also, that educational television assumes an often heavy burden of its own in television news, often providing the only television news service in rural parts of the United States. Here, too, financing always is the overriding factor and much has to be made out of little in the way of journalistic resources. Often, the news responsibility of public or educational television is turned over to schools of journalism associated with major universities, with many of the day-to-day functions of news coverage given to un-dergraduate or graduate students who work under the guidance of a few paid professionals.

As commercial and educational television stations come on the air in greater numbers, competition grows ever keener. This imposes on news personnel the ever increasing burden of coming up with fresh ideas in news coverage and presentation. Indeed, it was a public television station in San Francisco that pioneered a concept of news presentation that caused all kinds of havoc among commercial stations across the country in 1970, and thereby provides a lesson on how competition can work. For a long time, WCBS-TV and WNBC-TV, the flagship stations of the CBS and NBC television networks, dominated the local news scene in the New York City viewing area. The American Broadcasting Company's own flagship station, WABC-TV, went casting about toward the end of the 1960s for some way to crack that hammerlock on the ratings and the advertising revenues. Gradually, WABC-TV adapted its own version of the "Newsroom" concept put into practice by KQED.

In the format of the San Francisco station, reporters and editors sit around a newspaper-style copy desk as they report, analyze and discuss the stories they've covered that day.

Much leeway is allowed for individual personalities to interact with each other. The conversation often runs a range from witty to "put down" to downright argumentative. WABC-TV carried the idea a step further, collecting a group of individuals with whom almost anyone could identify in some way and throwing them together twice each night to chide, goad, induce and otherwise evolve a pair of newscasts that shoots to the opposite side of the spectrum from the traditional, anchorman-style TV newscast.

Called "Eyewitness News," the WABC-TV formula is to present a roomful of reporters, each of whom introduces and describes film clips of the story or stories he has covered that day. The "team" image is carefully projected by dressing the reporters in blue blazers with a Channel 7 crest. The on-air personalities are encouraged to enter into a free-swinging repartee, which in itself attracted much attention to WABC-TV's once languishing news operation. Naturally, there were grave reservations in many quarters, including the New York Times, which questioned on its television page whether the WABC-TV format diminishes or enhances effectiveness. They pointed out that while irreverence can be refreshing, it also can be stretched a bit too far to become supercilliousness. At one point, the Times went so far as to say that WABC-TV's "Eyewitness News" might better be called "Wiseguy News." Whatever its critical acclaim, or criticism, WABC-TV became more and more wedded to its new concept as its ratings went up sharply and its two key competitors swing around to their own versions of the "Eyewitness News" concept.

This, of course, is just one example of the great latitude to be found in television journalism. Originally, the "star" system prevailed at both the network and local levels, with networks and independent stations building their newscasts around one particular correspondent. NBC broke this mold when it teamed Chet Huntley and David Brinkley in a New York-Washington dual anchor arrangement that was taken up by many other organizations and adapted to their own capabilities and means. The "Eyewitness News" concept merges the anchorman into a sometime folksy, sometimes argumentative family image that obviously appeals to the young with its emphasis on a wide open style of news presentation.

Whatever the situation, television news is young and vibrant, given to and capable of enormous change and flexibility. The spur of competition cuts back and forth across the public and commercial broadcasting lines, encouraging people with imagination to seek out every more interesting ways to present news. It's a constant challenge, and a challenge that is renewed regularly by the development of new technical tools and the refinement of the old ones.

STILL PICTURES

Television is a pictorial or visual medium. In its infancy, television news placed heavy reliance on the use of still pictures. A quick look back will show how technology has changed in this area alone. In the early days, it was common practice to mount a glossy, 8 by 10 inch or larger photograph on an easel or some kind of stand and then shoot it with a studio camera while the newscast was on the air. These pictures filled the entire screen and were known as "easel shots," for the obvious reason, and also as "limbos," possibly because they removed the newscaster temporarily from sight and created a situation in which a voice from nowhere related the picture on the screen to the news. As the use of still pictures evolved, easel shots pretty much gave way to a system in which the quality was improved by transferring a spot news picture or photograph of someone in the news onto a 4 by 5 inch mat that was used in a projection device known as a telopticon. The picture itself is called a "telop," and it, too, takes up the entire screen when put on the air at the command of the director. Thirty-five millimeter slides also are widely used in television news and the Polaroid camera proved to be a big help, especially for small television news operations. A reporter can get still shots of whatever activity he is covering and take them back to the studio for immediate use on the air.

Recently, the still picture technique has undergone a steady process of refinement. Today, the demand for ever more sophisticated production values has given rise to the rear screen projection technique in which pictures are used on a screen of any desired size or shape which is built into the set, or stage, on which a newscast is produced. A projector on the studio floor throws a slide picture into the rear screen and the picture, in turn, is taken on command by a studio camera. It also is possible to run both film and video tape in the same R.P. screen.

Rear screen projection is popular because it offers wide flexibility. It is possible, for instance, to have the newscaster and the picture on the R.P. screen in the same shot. Perhaps there is some minute detail in a still picture that has special meaning in a news story. With rear screen, it is possible to have the newscaster step right up to the screen and point out the item of interest. It is equally practical to use some kind of visual device to single out the item and have that particular pointer thrown onto the screen by the R.P. projector. Similarly, it is possible to have the newscaster address the screen as a film is projected, with both again being picked up by the studio camera, then to move in with the camera to take the film on the R.P. screen as a full screen shot and thereby create some visual excitement by the movement of the camera. Many such visual "gimmicks" are possible and creative news personnel and graphic artists should constantly combine their specialties to bring out better ways to illustrate news and feature material.

A number of organizations, including the Associated Press and United Press International, provide news photo services that furnish the great bulk of the still pictures used in television news. These spot news pictures are transmitted from AP and UPI headquarters to subscribers over a facsimile hook-up. The facsimile paper is flimsy and easily wrinkled and, therefore, usually required some doctoring up

This Associated Press facsimile machine is receiving a National Hockey League action photo. (Courtesy Norman Goldman)

by the art department before the photo can be used on the air. It also is possible to buy 8 by 10 glossy duplicates of the facsimile photos, which can be cropped, embellished or touched up in any way that improves their quality and the substance they add to the telling of the news.

It is common practice in television news to build a library of head shots of personalities who figure regularly in the news and just as common to rely all too heavily on photos of people who are so well known that their names bring an image to almost everyone's mind. In many news operations now, it is considered unnecessary to use a picture of the president, for instance, every time he figures in a news story, which is frequently. Often it is possible, with a bit of imagination, to use the head shot of the familiar figure with another picture or illustration of some facet of the story that is being told, which is a technique that can take the curse off the use of an ordinary head shot.

Much the same kind of complaint holds true in the use of maps. Even more than common head shots, maps are the most overworked graphic device in television news. Unfortunately, newsmen and artists all too often use a map in willy-nilly fashion just to have some kind of visual for the story. If the location of a news story is genuinely important to telling that story, then time should be taken for the newsman preparing the story to get together with an artist to design a meaningful map. Here, again, the development of the rear screen technique has provided ways to enhance the visual interest of otherwise ordinary maps, a technique that is discussed later. The main point, however, is that a talented and creative artist or art department is of inestimable value in improving the look of any newscast.

TELEVISION NEWSFILM

In its infancy, television news was limited to the capabilities of the motion picture camera. Only a relative handful of professional cameramen had any experience in shooting film for newsreels and even their exposure had little application to a daily newsfilm operation because the theater newsreels were totally unconcerned with the immediacy of news. Long years were needed to train a corps of photographers who could strike the right balance between composing pictures and covering a fast-breaking news story. All too often, the early newscasts were little more than patchwork productions using anything and everything that had sprocket holes. It was the heyday of the press agent, whose investment in a few hundred feet of 16-millimeter film often was returned many times over both in network and local exposure. The nation was fed a fatty diet of water skiing and other zany antics, many of which were designed to promote some commerical venture. That sorry day in electronic journalism began to wane as television grew in popularity and leaders in the field began to sense the potential in news and, indeed, to live up to their responsibilities in this area.

Short silent film clips made up much of the television newsfilm shown on air in the early days. The next big step was to devise quick and practical ways to use the sound camera. Logistically, the problems wre enormous. Sound gear is bulky and awkward. Ordinarily it requires the full attention of one man to make certain the camera is recording sound properly while the cameraman concentrates on making pictures that not only are in focus but also will tell a story. Little by little, the major network and independent news organizations contributed to the development of full camera crews that can be available for round-the-clock news coverage. Today, a network news camera crew usually consists of as many as five men who can be assembled quickly and dispatched in great haste, are fast on their feet, resourceful, often willing to battle their way to the scene of an assignment and durable enough to get back to news headquarters with a respectable finished product. Normally, the network newsfilm crew is made up of a reporter, cameraman, sound man and an electrician. If the shooting assignment is in any way complicated, an assistant cameraman often is sent along to help. Usually, the entire job is put under the supervision of a news-oriented field producer, someone who can blend news judgment with production know-how. Obviously, close teamwork is an absolute necessity when so many individual specialists are involved in one assignment.

Among the major independent stations and network affiliates, staffing patterns vary according to need. More often than not, a newsfilm team is scaled down to the reporter, cameraman and sound man. The need for harmonious cooperation among the members of a news film team are obvious. They must work together, often traveling in a radio-equipped car, filming one event, dropping the film off for processing and speeding off to another job. Some of the news-conscious stations put five or more newsfilm teams into the field every day and each team usually handles three or four assignments every day. They must be flexible enough to be able to drop an assignment in the middle when a news emergency arises and then go back to pick up where they left off. By and large, the reporter is the one who has the decision-

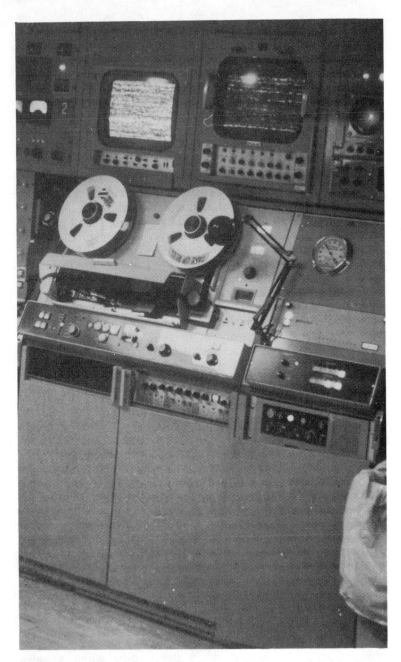

Modern video tape machine. (Courtesy Norman Goldman)

making power and the overall responsibility for getting the story on film and getting it right. He must understand both the editorial and technical problems of covering news on film and getting it on the air. Here, again, as in all aspects of broadcast journalism, the more a newsman understands about his medium and the greater industry and imagination he brings to his work, the more effective he is bound to be.

VIDEO TAPE

One of the most important advances that has come from the development of television technology is video tape. It is that long sought facility for recording picture and sound for immediate or subsequent playback. With video tape, the time consuming step of processing is eliminated. Picture and sound are recorded by electronic processes on magnetic tape. Once the recording is made, with electronic cameras feeding a video tape recorder, the tape can be rewound and played back in seconds, as anyone knows who has watched television coverage of sporting events. Beyond that inestimable advantage of immediacy, video tape also provides live quality picture and sound. In television programming today, live dramatic and entertainment programs are almost non-existent. It makes no sense to mount any kind of costly production live and run the risk of some mistake or accident on the air when the production can be recorded and misspoken lines or stage mishaps edited out so that the home viewer sees a perfect performance.

With its high fidelity picture and sound, video tape has made just as much of an impact on news as it has on the entertainment side of television. Newscasts rarely are recorded in advance because they must be left open for last-minute developments, but elements of the newscast are pre-recorded. The most recent development is to transfer any kind of complicated film piece to video tape before the newscast, a technique discussed in more detail later. An even more basic and far-reaching impact of video tape is the way it has helped to speed the delivery of film coverage of distant events to home viewers.

As is the case in radio, television loops and lines can be installed at any television station, thereby enabling that station to feed program material to another station or receiving point. This was always true. In the early days of television, however, the practice was restricted by available technology, which consisted of kinescope recording of material fed from another station. The kinescope process consisted simply of making motion picture film directly off the television tube. This was little help from the standpoint of time as the kinescope film had to be processed in the same manner as any other film and the loss of quality was enormous.

Because there was no way then to receive a picture and turn it around for immediate or even quick replay, the networks in the early days of television news were restricted largely to the hazardous practice of picking up news material from correspondents at affiliated stations or other originating points and using it live during the actual newscast. This system was threatened, primarily, by the possibility of telephone line failure, which occurred more than infrequently, to the public embarrassment of the anchorman and the private annoyance of all those behind the scenes. This system also reduced the producer's control over material that was put on air. In normal circumstances, where a newscast is put together and aired from one central point, New York or Washington, for instance, the producers and often the anchorman see everything before it is put on the air. They have authority to order a film or video tape recut to improve its editorial or pictorial content or, in fact, to drop the element entirely if it does not meet their editorial or production standards. On the other hand, when film, video tape or even live material is fed directly into a production on the air, the control largely is lost. The network producer can talk by telephone before the newscast with the affiliate newsman who has screened and cut the pictorial element, and the producer must decide whether or not to spend often substantial sums for that material only on the basis of what his associate at the switching point tells him. With the coming of video tape, those risks and uncertainties were largely eliminated. Today, live switches are infrequent.

On the coverage of major news stories and especially events that can be anticipated, the networks send their own news teams composed of associate producers, correspondents, cameramen, sound men, electricians and sometimes even their own film editors to establish a base of temporary operations at the network owned-and-operated station or affiliate nearest the scene of the event. From that point, the news team covers and makes as much film of the event as the producer needs, a decision that is determined by frequent telephone conferences among producers at network news headquarters and associate producers and correspondents at the scene. As this material is developed, either on film or video tape, telephone lines are ordered from the affiliate station to network headquarters. This material is taken in on video tape.

Ordinarily it is viewed by the producers either as it is "fed" in or shortly thereafter and the producers decide how much of it they want or need for any particular newscast. If the producer feels an important element of the story has been omitted, he can order the piece redone right then and there.

In addition to this kind of coverage, it is common for network news headquarters to ask an affiliate station to cover some news development in its area that would have national interest. Here, too, when time is an important factor, the affiliate would be asked to feed its material to news headquarters where it is recorded on video tape and subsequently edited to meet editorial and time requirements. When time is not so vital, the affiliate might simply be asked to film or tape the event and ship the material by air or some other form of transportation.

The other side of all this is that video tape is equally important to network affiliate and local television stations. An affiliate can record both program and news material for later playback and it is common practice for an affiliate to carry a major network newscast live at its normal time and then to recut and reuse portions of the newsfilm from that newscast in later local news productions. In the case of the independents, they have the option of receiving video tape as well as film prints from whatever syndicated news service they subscribe to. Indeed, the time lag of distributing newsfilm has been telescoped by the practice of leasing telephone lines and distributing syndicated material daily over those lines instead of shipping or mailing it.

When video tape arrived on the television scene, its great advantages were offset to some degree by the technical problems involved in editing it. A video tape technician often needed as much as 20 minutes to make a single splice or edit. Manual splicing still can take a lot of time under certain circumstances, although technological advantages come rapidly in the field of electronics and video tape now can be spliced automatically as quickly as film which, in the hands of a capable editor, is only a matter of seconds. Some of these advances and their application to news are discussed in greater detail in later chapters.

There remain today many places that cannot be reached with "live" broadcast equipment. Because of this, video tape and film seem destined for some time to come to share top billing as television news' foremost source of picture.

EXPANDING HORIZONS OF TELEVISION NEWS

The electronic technology responsible for the development and refinement of video tape in such a short time has rapidly closed the national and international communications gaps. The two developments do, in fact, go hand-in-hand. Where once the spanning of the United States by coaxial cable and microwave relay seemed a miracle of communications, now it is possible to bridge the oceans by communications satellites. Now, the sight and sound of news and general information can be bounced back and forth between continents and recorded on video tape, giving man still another opportunity to learn about and understand his fellow man in faraway places. Now, of course, that opportunity is immediate. Since the first communications satellite went up over the Atlantic in the 1960s, it has been possible for television viewers in all parts of the United States to witness events taking place in Western Europe and vice versa. Now, other oceans have been spanned and, from the communications standpoint, the world has drawn still closer. As more and more satellites are put to work, the enormous initial costs of using these facilities is reduced more and more, although the expenses still prohibit frequent use of them. Originally, satellite use charges ran in the neighborhood of $2,500 for a minimum transmission of ten minutes and $60 for every additional minute. This same scaling down of line costs is true in domestic transmission, although a major portion of the tremendous production costs of television news is devoted to these line charges. Within the confines of the competition, however, technological advances of any kind that cut the time lag between reporting an event and airing the coverage are welcome.

TELEVISION COVERAGE OF SPECIAL EVENTS

There are news events of such widespread interest and great importance that the television industry provides special, sustained coverage. To do this requires tremendous effort on the part of everyone involved, and the primary responsibility for this kind of activity falls, naturally, to the news department. For the anchorman and correspondents, it means long hours of deep study and preparation to acquire a familiarity with all the pertinent information and the minutiae of the event, everything that is or might be used to keep viewers well informed and interested. Producers are under a constant demand to come up with new and unique methods of presenting the event from every conceivable angle and in

Color technicians setting up color pickup equipment at the scene of a remote broadcast. (Courtesy CBS News)

inventive ways. For the technicians, it means a maximum effort to move all the necessary electronic gear from home base to the location of the event and to make sure it is installed, checked out and used properly. Major news organizations invest huge sums in "remote units," which usually are large conveyances converted into mobile television studios, control rooms and work rooms.

One obvious example of an event that requires this sort of special coverage is the quadrennial presidential nominating conventions which, after all the months and months of preparations, are 6- to 8-day affairs that consume television's attention almost completely. Outside the convention site, huge parking areas are taken over by the remote trucks that have converged on the scene of political history in the making from ali parts of the country. This, alone, is a major logistical problem for the individuals heading up the coverage for the various news organizations and those in charge for the two major political parties. If, for instance, a politician from California were expected to be nominated for the presidency at a convention in Boston, many California stations would want to be there to report the event. For the networks, which provide the bulk of the coverage and engage in fierce competition to outdo each other, no single remote truck could even begin to do the job. Instead, hundreds of tons of equipment are carried to the convention site in privately-owned and rented vehicles. The cost of this kind of coverage runs to many millions of dollars, but the outlays are essential from the twin standpoints of competition and public service.

With these maximum news coverage efforts, the networks are able to "stake out" or place reporters and remote units at every point in the convention city where news might be made. They bring with them all the equipment needed to originate "live" program material and to video tape and to film almost everything that is open to news coverage. But, with all the preparations and technical agility that can be brought to or invented at the scene, the end product depends mostly on the calibre of talent that does the actual broadcasting—the anchormen, correspondents, reporters, commentators and analysts who will cover the story and carry it to the nation and, increasingly, to other interested parts of the world. It is true that the men who appear on camera usually are back-stopped by teams of editorial and technical experts, but in the end they are the ones who must perform, who must tell the story accurately and interestingly. There is far more to it than meets the eye of the viewer in his easy chair.

A portable, wireless color TV camera in use at a remote pickup with CBS News Correspondent Mike Wallace. (Courtesy CBS News)

INVESTIGATIVE REPORTING

As television news expands and matures, there is a growing drive to push ever deeper into the area of investigative reporting. This is a time-honored function of journalism and a proper concern of the new medium. This kind of reporting does, however, pose unique problems for television. The newspaper reporter or magazine writer whose equipment is a brain, eyes and pad and pencil has a distinct advantage over the investigative reporter for television who, naturally, is trying to get his story on film or tape. It isn't easy, for instance, to conceal the sound camera and it is impossible to compel a subject with something to hide to sit still for a filmed or taped interview. That individual might under circumstances fortunate for the newsman be caught unexpectedly in a compromising statement captured on film, but if he is bright enough to work some major kind of swindle, the chances are he is devious enough to avoid hurting himself in front of television cameras. Similarly, it is difficult, although not impossible, for the television reporter to be on hand with his equipment when a crime is being committed or at that precise moment when a crooked politician is duping the public. To bring that off on camera requires a combination of good investigation, good planning and good luck.

Beyond this basic limitation, however, there is a broad area left to the industry and ingenuity of the television newsman. When he comes on a story that must be told, he may have to resort to the more traditional techniques of exposure, perhaps documenting his case wherever possible with still pictures and other illustrations. In the end, he may have to fall back on the device of telling the story himself and quoting or not quoting his sources. The chief consideration always is that utmost care must be taken in checking out such an important and possibly dangerous story before it is brought to the public's eye. Much responsibility rests with the television reporter and his organization. Unquestionably, there are those who violate the public's trust and should be called upon to account for their deeds. In a complex society, one that is utterly beyond the mental grasp of many, an influential medium such as television has much hard work to do to educate and involve the citizen in the world about him.

Although it doesn't fall under the category of investigative reporting, it is interesting to note the experiments taking place around the United States in which television has taken up the task of providing live coverage of local government. Mostly, this means broadcasting meetings of city councils and similar governing bodies. Early indications are that people starved for interesting programs to watch can be caught up in this world that many did not know exists. If indeed this proves to be a new trend in television viewing, it could work terrible hardships for some politicans who have counted on the low profile as they amassed and employed power.

THE TELEVISION DOCUMENTARY

Still another regular function of television news in which the broadcaster has a primary role is the television documentary, or an extended look at a particular problem or facet of our society. There is, however, no rule of thumb to define the participation of the regular anchorman or correspondent. By and large, documentaries are produced by the news department of a network or independent station. Because of the nature of the technique, however, documentaries more often than not are the creation of one or two trained newsmen who have spent great amounts of time looking into the subject on which they are reporting. For this reason, alone, it is almost impossible for a correspondent who holds down a regular anchor spot or covers a regular news assignment to break away from his normal routine to devote himself to the preparation of a documentary.

It is not uncommon for major documentary productions to take up to six months or even longer in preparation. If, for instance, an hour of broadcasting time has been set aside for a report in depth on a situation in some foreign country, much time must be spent in travel and location shooting of film. In cases where a featured network anchorman or correspondent is to be used, often the camera crew and production team will get all the preparations out of the way so that the correspondent has only to spend a few days on the scene to carry out his role. This normally means the correspondent has little or no part in writing the original script. There are those correspondents who insist on writing or rewriting extensively and making their own personalities felt in the creation of one of these studies and must then make time to participate more fully in the documentary production. Others are content to step in, pick up a finished script and read it on air or, more likely, during the taping session. Here again, decisions like these boil down to a question of personalities and sometimes to a question of the budgetary considerations involved. At the local level, documentaries require much work to be done well and to make a substantial contribution to understanding, but the fact that the job can be done locally often makes the active participation of the top anchorman much more practical and feasible. In terms of the prestige of the station, it is often mandatory for that person to bring the documentary to the public.

There is, and hopefully always will be, ample room in television news, whether at the level of the daily newscast or the creation of an important documentary, for much give-and-take among the news personnel. Often, the best work is the result of the creative blending of many ideas by people working toward the same goal of meaningful journalism.

CHAPTER 8

The TV Newscast

Editorially, the steps taken to prepare for the radio newscast are repeated and expanded in television news. At the beginning of each day the broadcaster must "read in" to familiarize himself with current events, then he usually sits down with his producers and other associates to talk over the pictorial material available that day. Here, again, the need for understanding and close cooperation is great, regardless of the level involved. An extremely forceful personality can undertake too much of a role in each phase of the broadcast—planning, writing and producing. Somewhere along the way, some vital role must suffer when this happens. At the other extreme is the newscaster who gets by only on voice and appearance and makes no effort to participate in his production, other than to air it. At the local level, an anchorman is required to perform production and editorial chores because the staff often is limited and there's no one else to do the various jobs. At the network level, the newscaster must establish a workable relationship with many specialists involved in getting his production on air. With the expansion of the staff, the newscaster becomes dependent on more people and they, in turn, on him. Logic normally dictates that pleasant relationships lead to closer cooperation and a better product.

THE "LINE-UP"

It is common practice in network operations for the editorial staff—the newscaster, producers, editors and writers—to work from a "line-up" or preliminary outline of the day's production. It is not a hard and fast schedule, but rather a guide to how much time is devoted to each portion of the newscast and what elements might be included. In most cases, someone in a position of authority arrives at the station first and takes a survey of what newsfilm and video tape are available for that day's production. He might distribute a list to the entire editorial and production staff to begin to coordinate the day's effort.

In the case of a major network news production, the team of experts assigned to that particular newscast usually is given an entire work day of eight or more hours to prepare only that newscast. The anchorman ordinarily has ample time to familiarize himself with the day's news and the illustrative material available so that he can take an interest in and often a hand in planning the newscast and editing the film and tape, to write as little or as much of the newscast as he wishes and to rehearse and time his material. The idea is that a network newscast is an expensive proposition and every effort should be made to make it as smooth and flawless as possible.

What is true of the anchorman also holds true for the producers, associated producers, editors and writers. Each has an entire work day to prepare and to perform his activity in the most professional way. From the original list of available pictorial material, the preliminary line-up often is drawn several hours before airtime. By this time, the producer has a firmer line on the film and tape he wants to use and an editor has spent several hours reading the wire service reports, newspapers and perhaps the cables from overseas and other correspondents. They block out the newscast as it begins to take shape. Perhaps the editorial and production teams will be called in to discuss the line-up at that stage, or it might be that the writers are given specific stories to handle.

It should be noted here that while the function of the radio news writer has largely been assumed by the newscaster, himself, network television news productions still are complex enough to require the service of several writers to assist most anchormen. It is true that the amount of time for "live" copy, the material read on camera by the newscaster, usually is far less than that devoted to film and tape. Still, news changes constantly and often the long planned film and tape elements in a newscast are thrown out at the last minute to make room for something later or more important, and an anchorman simply can't handle the details of a late writing assignment and the broadcasting function, too.

When the line-up is drawn, assignments are made in as nearly final form as the nature of news allows. It is decided then what portions of the newscast the anchorman himself will write, and with the actual writing assignment goes the responsiblility for devising and ordering art work to illustrate various elements within the newscast.

A certain amount of time must be given over to so-called "tell" stories, those items for which there is no film or video tape. In consultation with the director, the writer may elect to use a spot news shot from one of the wire services, or a map or perhaps even a cartoon if the story lends itself to that kind of treatment. In addition to the "tell" stories, the anchorman and writers are given specific assignments for leading into the film and tape available. They assume responsibility for viewing that material and making certain the introductions are proper.

As the hours rush by, the editorial and pictorial content often change radically enough to require complete revision of the line-up. Now, the producer and editor who made the original line-up must coordinate all the information they have about changes and make certain everyone involved in every given function is aware of the changes as they affect the various members of the editorial and production teams.

There are, of course, many variations on the line-up method of operating and that's the way it should be. An independent station with a small crew putting a newscast together faces entirely different problems and in such cases the news personnel must refine their own system according to needs.

Whether its a local newscast or a major network production, it generally is good practice to make copies of the final format of the production, as much, that is, as any newscast ever is entirely "locked in," even on the air. Allowing for those on-air changes that sometimes become necessary, a general guide to the planned execution of the newscast can help all members of the production and editorial teams stay on top of their responsibilities until the program is off the air. When the line-up appears in final form, it normally reflects the time factors and visual elements, without any detailed editorial information. Following is a more or less typical line-up for a 30-minute newscast:

X.Y.Z. EVENING NEWS, WEDNESDAY, OCTOBER 10

1. OPEN & ANNOUNCE	16-4-	:30	7:00:00 - 7:00:30
2. LIVE		:45	7:00:30 - 7:01:15
3. PRES. MITCHELL	VT-8	2:15	7:01:15 - 7:03:30
4. LIVE		:15	7:03:30 - 7:03:45
5. FIRST COMMERCIAL (BLANK OIL CO.)	VT-10	1:00	7:03:45 - 7:04:45

6. LIVE		1:00	7:04:45 - 7:05:45
7. VIET NAM FILM (SMITH)	16-4- 16-6	3:00	7:05:45 - 7:08:45
8. LIVE		:20	7:08:45 - 7:09:05
9. SEN. JONES INTVU (GREEN)	VT-8	2:40	7:09:05 - 7:11:45

---

10. SECOND COMMERCIAL (GULPO DOG FOOD)	VT-10	1:00	7:11:45 - 7:12:45

---

11. LIVE		:15	7:12:45 - 7:13:00
12. PLANE CRASH VO	16-4	:30	7:13:00 - 7:13:30
13. LIVE		:15	7:13:30 - 7:13:45
14. F.A.A. FILM (O'BRIEN)	16-4- 16-6	3:10	7:13:45 - 7:16:55
15. LIVE		1:05	7:16:55 - 7:18:00

---

16. THIRD COMMERCIAL (PROMO: X.Y.Z. NET. COMEDY HOUR)	VT-10	1:00	7:18:00 - 7:19:00

---

17. LIVE		1:15	7:19:00 - 7:20:15
18. BRITISH TRAFFIC (PIERCE)	VT-8	2:15	7:20:15 - 7:22:30
19. LIVE		:30	7:22:30 - 7:23:00
20. CALIFORNIA POLITICS (ARTHUR)	16-2- 16-4	1:45	7:23:00 - 7:24:45
21. LIVE		:15	7:24:45 - 7:25:00

---

22. FOURTH COMMERCIAL (BLANK COFFEE)	VT-10	1:00	7:25:00 - 7:26:00

---

23. LIVE		:10	7:26:00 - 7:26:10

24. PITTSBURGH FILM (BROWN)		2:00 7:26:10 - 7:28:10
	16-4	
25. LIVE (G'NITE)	16-6	:20 7:28:10 - 7:28:30

26. FIFTH COMMERCIAL	VT-10	1:00 7:28:30 - 7:29:30
(BLANK SOFT DRINK)		

27. CLOSE & ANNOUNCE	16-4	:30 7:29:30 - 7:30:00

Now, let's go back over the hypothetical line-up and take it apart. Item number 1 is the standard or fixed opening or signature. Whether it is a network or local production, there ordinarily is a set way to identify the newscast. In our illustration, we'll say the opening has an animated film, designated by the numerals 16-4, which means that it is a 16-millimeter sound film and is to be run into the newscast on projector number 4. Perhaps the opening uses the day's date or other non-news matter that would be read by a staff announcer rather than the anchorman or newscaster himself. The opening should run a standard time, which naturally must be subtracted from the overall time of the production.

The 12 separate numbers marked with the designation "live" indicate those portions of the production in which the newscaster is on camera and seen and heard. Sometimes he will appear briefly, as in numbers 4, 8, 11, 13, 21 and 23. In those instances, he ordinarily would introduce a visual element or lead into a commercial or promotional announcement. The longer "live" sections, as in numbers 6, 15 and 17, indicate places in which the newscaster has at least a little time to cover some of the news for which there is no film or video tape.

COMMERCIALS AND PROMOTIONAL ANNOUNCEMENTS

The commercial and promotional announcements, numbers 5, 10, 16, 22 and 26, are important elements of any newscast. The commercials, of course, pay the bills for the news operations. The promotional announcements, or "promos," perform several related functions. They are made by television stations and networks to promote other productions either within the news department or for the entertainment side of the operation. Promotional material also is supplied to stations and networks by various charitable, medical or governmental agencies that seek private funds or offer various helpful services to viewers. The normal practice in commercial broadcasting, of course, is to sell several minutes' worth of advertising in every production, including newscasts. Often, those positions within a production are kept open by inserting a "promo" when no commercial sale has been made. In network operations, the common practice is to make a newscast or other production into what is known as a "participating" program in which the network designates several specific time segments within the production where promotional announcements are scheduled with the understanding that the affiliated stations are permitted to sell local advertising and insert it locally by cutting out of the network promo, then rejoining the network production when the message is finished. Networks try to expedite this practice by inserting a signal, known as Epps Cue, in the upper right-hand part of the screen ten seconds before they take a promo. Even with this precaution, missed cues and erratic timing often result in some strange phenomena along the network lines as stations cut out too early or rejoin a little late. It seems to be just one of the hazards of network operations.

Throughout the television industry, commercials and promos now are done almost entirely on either film or video tape. The day of the "live" commercial, with its often memorable goofs, is gone. There just is no need for advertisers today to spend all kinds of money and take the risks involved in trying to do it live.

It should be noted here that ordinarily the final line-up would specify exactly what the commercial or promotional messages are in any given newscast and their exact placement within that production. This is a worthy precaution against some inept juxtaposition with a news item. All too often situations arise in which, for instance, the final news item before a commercial for some rich and luxurious kind of food might be a story dealing with hunger or even starvation. A quick check of the commercial line-up early in the production phase can avoid such on-the-air embarrassment and even a late check of the final line-up can lead to some kind of rearrangement that would get around such a troublesome and unnecessary transition.

FILM AND TAPED INSERTS

It is generally helpful if the final line-up specifies whether pictorial elements are recorded on film or video tape. This

114

serves as a double check, usually, because the production team has spent their work day prior to air time screening the various pictorial elements, making precise notes on the timing of each element, the in-cues and out-cues and possible pitfalls to be avoided. In the final production, it is the responsibility of the director to put the newscast on the air in professional fashion. In network production, he is in charge of a technical team consisting of an associate director who is his direct assistant and helps with various cues, a technical director who runs a complicated control board and on cue from the director actually activates the various film and video tape projectors and studio cameras, and an audio engineer who is responsible for balancing the microphones, film and tape audio levels so that they sound as nearly perfect as possible when the newscast is on the air.

Often, an associate director and a production assistant, and perhaps even an editor or producer, check the running time as the production is on the air. Again, in network operations, this is a prime consideration because a production that runs over its scheduled time will be clipped off the air at whatever stage it happens to be. Thus, a close check of time enables the production crew to advise the newscaster to speed up his reading, to slow it down, to add fill copy or drop an item, whatever is needed to adjust to time requirements. At the local level, strict timing is not quite as important and the manpower available to check it is limited. At either level, the more accurate a final line-up can be made, the better it can serve as a quick reference for the technical and production staffs.

It makes good sense, also, to put a brief "slug," or word of identification, on each pictorial element and to provide a double check by inserting the name of the correspondent or reporter. For example, the number 3 item, slugged "Pres. Mitchell VT," should be easily understood. It might be an excerpt from a presidential news conference, or a White House statement on some issue of the day, delivered in person by the president and running to two minutes and 15 seconds of video tape. On the other hand, item number 7, is identified with a rather more general slug of "Viet Nam Film." To avoid possible confusion, the name of the correspondent or reporter can be used.

The designations, 16-4—16-6, after the film slug and reporter's name indicates that a so-called "double projector" film piece is involved. This means that film from two separate projectors is to be integrated on air. This technique is routine and is discussed in detail later.

Line-up number 9 is an interview recorded on video tape, in which Correspondent Green questioned Senator Jones on some aspect of the situation in Viet Nam. Since there is another report from Viet Nam in the production, it is entirely logical to lead quickly from one element to the other. In the example, we'll assume that Correspondent Green has done his own "wrap-around," which would be his own brief introduction and sign-off. Such an interview often permits the production staff to format the newscast in such a way that there is no need to return to the anchorman to introduce a commercial or promotional announcement. It is just as common, however, for interviews to be edited in such a way that they end on a statement by the subject. In these cases, it is usually necessary to "tag" or "button" the interview by having the newscaster return on camera to say something appropriate to the subject or even to repeat the name of the interview subject so as to round the interview off and provide a smooth transition into the commercial or promotional message.

SILENT PICTURE AND VOICE OVER

Item number 12 brings us to still another of the basic techniques of television: the silent film or video tape with voice over (often designated with the abbreviation of VO). When called for in an editorial line-up, voice-over copy usually means the newscaster, himself, will do the voicing. In the strictest sense of the term, every picture used is a voice-over because someone in the field or in the newsroom has prepared a narration and someone has given voice to that narration and put it over the picture. The various methods of handling the voice-over are explained in the next chapter, but the point to be made regarding the line-up is that this system of television reporting can be used widely to illustrate a story in its own right or to set up still another element within the newscast. In the illustration, the producer elects to run in 30 seconds of film of the aftermath of a plane crash. In this case, the film serves the dual purpose of illustrating the story and also sets up an interview with a spokesman for the Federal Aviation Administration, once again combining common elements into a smoothly flowing newscast.

"STRUCTURING" A NEWSCAST

There are as many ways to structure a television newscast as there are news and pictorial elements. The imagination of the production and editorial staffs and the technical capabilities of the station impose the only limits. The newscast must be a flexible vehicle that can truly mirror the fast-changing news, itself. More often than not, the flow of the day's news is what ultimately determines the structure of that day's newscast. This is generally true in all daily handling of the news, whether on television, radio or in the newspaper. One day there will be a particular story of such overriding importance that almost all of the newscast will be devoted to telling as much as can be told in the time available about that one story. From the telling of the basic story, there might be interview to bring out certain aspects and sidebar or related items to throw even more light on the big story. Then, another day will find the editorial staff digging for a leadworthy news story because the day's run of news adds up only to bite and snippets, with nothing of standout importance. Whichever the case, the objective in television news is to put together a production in which whatever news there is, is told well and interestingly in a way in which words and pictures blend as naturally and smoothly as possible. Sometimes this is utterly impossible without wrestling some of the elements into place. Again, it is more satisfactory in these situations to break the wrestling hold and let the anchorman use his performing ability to carry off a complete stop, and then to proceed to another, unrelated item.

The fourth section of the illustration, items 17 through 21, could be what is known as a "catch-all" section, one unlike the previous segments in the sense that there is no real relationship from picture to picture or item to item, or only an incidental relationship with no central theme running through the section, such as the Viet Nam section or the plane crash segment. In item number 17, for instance, the newscaster might tick off three or four items of international news, each running to 15 or 20 seconds. The remaining 15 seconds in the item are given over to an introduction to the film. In cases like this, it would be advisable to put together a minute-long package of news ending, if at all possible, on an item from Britain. Obviously, this would lead the viewer naturally into the geographical area in which the upcoming filmed report is located. When this cannot be done, the practical answer again is simply to break off completely from what went before and go directly to the new item.

For purposes of illustration, let's say the British film is a report on that nation's efforts to cope with modern traffic congestion in London. Coming out of the British film, there's a relatively brief live section in item number 19. Those 30 seconds must be used to transport the viewer easily from the subject of highways to a political development in California, with no relationship between the filmed elements. On a day when the luck of the news is running high, there just might be a suitable domestic political item that can be told quickly and used also to bridge between the British film and the California film. If not, the writer just must cover the distance as gracefully as possible.

Many TV news producers still try to save the final segment of the newscast for some sort of lighter item whenever possible. This is something of a carry-over from the radio news use of the "kicker" or "brightness" item and perhaps its staying power indicates merit in the practice. In item number 24, then, let's say that Correspondent Brown has unearthed some sort of fun-and-games feature in Pittsburgh which the production staff has screened and decided is worth two minutes at the end of today's newscast. Ordinarily, a light item such as this shouldn't require much time to set up. As a matter of fact, the quicker the introduction in instances of this kind, the less likely it is that the anchorman might step on some aspect of the film story, or cause unnecessary repetition.

After the "brightener" film, the newscaster would have just a bit of time perhaps to add his own wry comment on the final item or merely to say good night. Either way, it is good practice to leave a little leeway, at least ten seconds, to make whatever adjustments might be necessary to get the production off the air on time.

The final item, number 27, is the standard closing which, like the opening, would be fixed in form and time as a readily identifiable signature for the production.

When at last the anchorman is in place before the camera and the production and technical personnel are in their places on the studio floor and in the control room, the line-up serves its final function as a guide to the actual running time of the production. The associate director or whoever is responsible for keeping check on the running time uses the line-up for a quick spot check of whether the newscast is running too fast, too slow or, if all the planning has worked out, right on time.

CHAPTER 9

Elements of the TV Newscast

Important as it is for the newscaster to be familiar with the techniques of news gathering and with the developments of each day, it is equally vital for him to understand the technical aspects of television news. Television news still is a young and often experimental medium, and editorial and production personnel try constantly to find new and better ways to blend journalism and technology in the hope of achieving superior ways to communicate. When a system does work well for a station or a network, it usually is the result of diligent application of a well-developed sense of news values superimposed on an understanding of what television can and cannot do.

"SPLITTING" THE DIFFERENCE

From the standpoint of television production, perhaps the most apparent difference between radio and television news is the script. The radio script is nondescript; it takes any form the newscaster prefers. He is free to exercise that option because, for the most part, he is the only one who needs a script during a newscast. Ordinarily, the television script must be made in at least five copies so that members of the editorial and production teams can follow the production word for word and instruction by instruction. The television script is divided in half vertically, with production instructions on one side and the news copy on the other. Into the **video** column, always on the left-hand side of the page, goes a brief and precise description of what should be happening at that second. If the newscaster is **on camera** at the time, the script indicates this in some standard way. Often, the use of the newscaster's name or just his initials in the video column will be the signal that the camera is to be on him at that stage of the production. Then, again, it could be that the newscaster might have a visual element with him at a given moment in a **rear screen projection** setting. This would be indicated on the script with the usual designation for the newscaster, plus the

CBS News Correspondent John Hart, shown on the Morning News set, with a base map on the rear screen. (Courtesy Norman Goldman)

indication of the visual (RP) and a "slug" or caption to identify the picture.

For the purpose of illustration, let's take our hypothetical newscast to the next logical step and give it an anchorman by the name of Dave Johnson. Some might choose to be very formal and indicate his appearances with the full designation of **Johnson On Camera**, or, less formally, **Johnson O-C**. Since these things tend to become regularized, the full designations soon give way to abbreviations, in this case **DJ-OC** and perhaps even just the initials of DJ will be sufficient to signal the control room company that it's Dave Johnson's time to shine.

In the second instance, where Dave Johnson will appear in tandem with a still photograph on the rear screen, the script probably would show the designation **DJ & RP**. Then, to take the illustration to its final step, let's say the still picture in question is a head shot of someone in the day's news. For purposes of safety, it is wise to name the individual or, in the case of a spot news picture, to describe it in a word in parentheses under the RP designation.

Since the development of rear screen projection, it has become popular to employ visual gimmicks to give a still picture at least some movement and added interest. For instance, if a story is to be illustrated by a map, the map itself might appear on the rear screen as soon as the newscaster launches into that particular story. Then, a graphic symbol can be thrown onto the screen to pinpoint the place where the action took place. The symbol might be a cross of some kind, a drawing that represents an explosion, or the outline of an airplane or ship, or whatever fits the story. Sometimes the name of a city or town will be used, or a one-word caption that characterizes that particular development in the news. This added element must be indicated on the script at the point at which the newscaster or writer feels it should appear. In TV news jargon, this symbolic embellishment of a map or anything else is referred to in various terms, such as a **pop on** or even as a **splat**. The terminology isn't as important as an understanding among all concerned of what is supposed to happen. It is entirely possible, too, to bring a map or still picture onto the screen as the anchorman refers to it rather than at the very start of an item.

Earlier, there was a brief discussion of the use of full-screen still pictures, such as slides and telops. These, too,

Outline of the Navajo Indian Reservation used as a "pop-up" or "splat" on a map. (Courtesy Norman Goldman)

must be indicated on the script so that the control room and production crews know what is going to happen and when. Here, too, it is wise to underline the direction with that brief description of the picture to avoid any uncertainty.

It should also be noted here that a series of still pictures sometimes is used to illustrate a story for which no film or tape is available. In such cases, it is imperative that the still shots are adequately identified, either by numbers or slugs, so that the director and other members of the production and control room crews and understand clearly what goes where and when.

Then, too, there are several different technical methods of proceeding from one picture to the next, which the newscaster or writer can suggest to the director. In some instances, it is better simply to change directly from one still to the next. This ordinarily would be indicated by the video column instruction to **take** the particular **RP, telop** or **slide**. In other instances, there might be a more dramatic visual effect by dissolving from one picture to the next, which is to say that one picture is slowly faded out and the next is slowly faded in. In local news operations, the decision of how to handle a change of pictures often is left to the newscaster or writer. In network operations, where specialization is the rule, the decision ordinarily would be made in conjunction with the director or left entirely to his judgment.

VIDEO TAPE AND FILM CUES

Precise instructions about video tape and film are just as necessary as the proper designation of still photographs on the television news script. In using tape or film, however, there is an additional technical consideration. Video tape machines normally require seven seconds to stabilize to reproduce a picture, while 16 millimeter film projectors take from three to four seconds to reach proper running speed. When the script is written, the director uses a stopwatch to measure the proper time for him to give his command to the technical director or, if he is operating his own control board, to punch up the element to be used. In TV jargon, these critical points in the script are known as video tape **roll cues** or film **hit cues**. For smooth production, they are inviolable.

It is common to make all kinds of changes in a television news script right up to and often during broadcast. The one thing that must be coordinated absolutely between the newscaster and the director is any change in a roll cue or hit cue. If the director does not know when to roll a tape or hit a film, he either will "up-cut" the pictorial element, which means he gets it on air seconds late and loses the first few words, or else he "catches some black," which means the roll cue or hit cue was delivered too early and the screen goes blank for however many seconds are required for the tape or film to come up. That blank screen is called "black." It is particularly important for the newscaster to realize the importance of roll and hit cues and to avoid any temptation to change copy or ad-lib as he's introducing tape or film.

VIDEO TAPE AND FILM INTRODUCTIONS

When the newscaster or writer introduces a video tape or filmed insert, he must be careful, as was pointed out in connection with audio tape, to avoid any duplication of the wordage or information on the taped or filmed report. Again, this means that the script writer must look at the visual element and make notes of its content to avoid "stepping on" that report in any way. Often a correspondent in the field will send in a complete script with his film. Many major news operations take the precaution of having a verbatim transcript made of taped and filmed material and distributed before broadcast to everyone concerned so as to avoid duplication. While it is helpful to have either a script or transcript, it still is wise for the newscaster or writer to screen the visual before writing into it to double check that no changes were made for production purposes or just to "get the feel" of the picture story, which often helps in writing an introduction.

In cases where no scripts or transcripts are available, it is not merely prudent but imperative for a writer to screen a film or tape before preparing the introduction. Obviously, no one can safely write into a report with no knowledge of what that report says or shows, and few mistakes are more apparent and make a newscaster look more foolish than for him to say something and have a reporter or interview subject come right up on tape or film and say the same thing. The few extra minutes it takes to screen tape or film are well worth the investment. In news operations where scripts and transcripts are not available, it also is good practice for the newscaster to know what the taped or filmed report is all about just in case of a technical failure on the air. The notes he made or his memory of what he saw can serve as protection if a tape machine malfunctions or film breaks on the air, and he suddenly finds himself facing a hot camera. Instead of sitting there "with egg on his face," he can gracefully excuse away the failure and go on to tell the sense of the report so that the audience is not left to wonder about it.

As far as the script is involved, the video tape and film instructions are relatively few and quite specific. Ordinarily, video tape consists of feeds taken in before broadcast, studio interviews, syndicated material or, increasingly, complicated filmed reports that are transferred to tape before broadcast for the convenience of the director and for added safety of production on the air. Tapes in these categories would be complete with sound track and could be indicated on the script simply with the story slug and the designation of VT. The total running time in minutes and seconds should be noted, along with the in cue and the out cue, or some indication of what the final sound is before the tape runs out. When silent video tape is called for, it might be indicated by the notation of VT (SIL) and its running time. Film ordinarily is designated as SIL, for silent, or SOF, for sound on film, or as a double projector report. The latter often is designated simply as DBL or else by the numerical designations of the projectors that will be used to put the film on the air.

SILENT TAPE AND FILM

There are many occasions when the production staff will want to use either video tape or film for picture only, in which case the sound track, if one exists, either will be erased physically or held off the air electronically. In these situations, the newscaster or someone else must speak the narration, or **voice over**. Writing the voice over is perhaps the most demanding aspect of scripting television news because, in many cases, it requires that the voice match the picture precisely.

There are several practical ways to handle the voice over. The fundamental move, of course, is for the individual responsible for making the cut in either film or video tape to view all the picture available to find out what is in it and thus be able to select the best shots. It might be that the editorial staff is looking for a 30-second cut of silent film to be drawn from a 400-foot roll, or roughly 12 minutes of film. If the newscaster, himself, plans to cut the film and write his own voice-over and has ample time to do it, he would screen all the film with a stopwatch in hand, making notes of what each scene contains and how long it runs in the original, uncut version. Obviously, if he has almost 24 times as much film as is needed, substantial editing is required. After the screening, the newscaster would review his notes, select the most dramatic or illustrative sequences and have them put together in what he feels is the most useful way. He might give the film editor, or whoever will do the actual splicing of film or tape, a rundown or shot list noting each scene he wants to use and how much time he wants to give it in the desired sequence. Then, with those notes, he can sit down immediately with the picture fresh in mind to write his voice over.

One variation of that technique, especially practical when someone else directs the film editing, is to wait until the 30-second film clip has been put together to screen the finished version with the stopwatch and make a rundown or shot list at that time. Quite another technique allows the newscaster to screen the uncut film. Then with a clear idea of what shots he wants to use, the writer can return to his typewriter to write the narration. After it is written, the newscaster times each sequence and makes notes of the times. The script with his timings then can be turned over to a film editor to cut the film to match the script.

As a further illustration of the various techniques, a voice-over in a well-equipped news operation can be handled by letting the newscaster screen the film, write the narration and record it on sprocketed audio tape. The tape, itself, can be turned over to a film editor to run it through a synchronizer, or film measuring device, while he lays in picture to match the voice. The sprocketed tape and silent film can then be played simultaneously on the air as a double projector film report. Practically speaking, these various techniques apply more readily to silent film than to video tape which is so much more cumbersome to edit unless automatic editing equipment is available.

Voice-over copy can be used for two distinct purposes. Occasionally, when the background of a story in the news is fairly familiar to viewers or readily understandable, it is possible to use silent film only for visual interest. In these instances, the narration relates only in a general way to the picture on the screen and there is no real need for the voice over to match the picture scene for scene. The picture, then, is self-explanatory. Much more common is the use of silent film in a precise manner in which the voice-over copy explains the news story. In these instances, it is necessary for tight synchronization of word and picture. If the newscaster or writer has prepared his copy carefully, it should be easy for the newscaster to find his words falling exactly on the right pictures. In cases where the narration has been written for the newscaster, it might take a second reading against the film to get it down exactly and to polish off any rough edges. If for any reason the newscaster is unsure of his picture or timing, he might pencil in cue words in the audio column or, in fact, ask the writer to do that while writing the narration.

Under normal circumstances, voice-over films in newscasts are run for relatively brief time periods, usually 30 seconds to a minute or so. In rare instances when silent film is particularly good and the production staff decides to give it more time (and the facilities are available), it is wise to let the newscaster pre-record the narration on audio tape to be run as a double projector during the newscast so as not to overburden him with the details of hitting a voice over precisely in the middle of a production. Still another consideration in the preparation of a narration is to allow for inherent drama to carry itself. From time to time, a cameraman is just at the right place at the right time and might record on film a moment of high emotional or pictorial intensity. The newscaster should realize immediately that here is a picture that speaks for itself. At best, he should merely prepare his viewers for what is coming and then fall quiet. The role of the narrator always must be to help the viewer understand what he is seeing on his screen.

EDITING AND SCRIPTING SILENT FILM

For purposes of discussion, let's place a cameraman at the scene of an automobile race in which a spectacular accident took place. Our cameraman was assigned to shoot what could only be expected to be a routine event and we'll say he filmed the action in one 400-foot roll of silent color film. The cameraman made all the usual establishing scenes but made no attempt to film the entire race. He was shooting, however, when the accident occurred as the cars were going into the home stretch. After the film has been processed, our newscaster is seated in the screening room with his pad, pencil, and stopwatch. A film editor threads up the 12-minute roll of film and starts the projector. Making sure his watch is starting at zero, he makes notes of the scenes and cumulative timing, like this:

Crowd in stands	:20
Cars away	:55
Into first turn	1:30
Cars in straight-away	3:45
Crowd standing	4:10
Cars in turn	4:35
No. 3 car in trouble	4:45
No. 3 car in skid	4:50

No. 3 car hits barrier	5:00
No. 3 car turns over	5:40
No. 3 car rolls twice	5:50
Ambulance to scene	6:10
Driver out of no. 3 car	6:35
Driver waves and walks away	8:10
Crowd looks on	8:30
Wreckage towed to infield	8:50
Cars resume race	9:20
3 cars in finish drive	9:45
Across finish line	10:15
Winner gets trophy	11:15
Crowds disperse	12:00

Now, the film has been screened, from the first to the last frame. Everyone agrees it's a spectacular crash, good enough picture to rate one whole minute on an otherwise busy news day. Even so, that's still only one-twelfth of the film that was shot, so the newscaster will have to be quite selective in making his cut. He goes back over his rundown and figures what he wants. Almost everyone in the area has visited the county fair grounds at one time or another, so the newscaster decides to save time by going right into the race and action. From the original 12 minutes of film and a stopwatch timing of every sequence, the newscaster and his film editor agree they'll cut the piece like this:

Cars in straight-away	:05
No. 3 car in skid	:05
No. 3 car hits barrier	:05
No. 3 car turns over	:15
No. 3 car rolls twice	:20
Crowd standing	:02
Driver steps from car	:04
Driver waves and walks off	:04

Since the newscaster has seen the film and made a precise shot list of each scene in sequence and how long it is to run, there's nothing to prevent him from going right back to his typewriter to write both the introduction and his voice over, which might turn out to be something like this:

VIDEO	AUDIO
DJ & RP	AT THE COUNTY FAIR
(FAIR GROUNDS)	GROUNDS THIS AFTERNOON,

AUTO RACE FILM
DJ-VO ⅛:00

A CROWD OF THREE-THOUSAND TURNED OUT FOR THE LABOR DAY ONE-HUNDRED MILE STOCK CAR RACE. THE FANS GOT MORE THAN THEY BARGAINED FOR IN THIS YEAR'S EVENT...AN EIGHT-CAR CONTEST:

THROUGH THE FIRST EIGHTY-FIVE LAPS IT WAS ROUTINE...ALMOST A DULL AFFAIR.

THEN, EVERYTHING CHANGED. DRIVER STAN SWIFT'S NUMBER THREE CAR GOT INTO TROUBLE.

SWIFT COULDN'T STRAIGHTEN OUT...AND HE BROUGHT THE CROWD TO ITS FEET AS HE HIT THE METAL AND CONCRETE WALL.

FOR A WHILE, IT LOOKED BAD FOR THE POPULAR LOCAL DRIVER AS HIS CAR BOUNCED OFF THE BARRIER AND WENT INTO A SPEC-TACULAR SERIES OF ROLLS.

(PAUSE :07)

THE OTHER SEVEN CARS HAD STOPPED AND THE AMBULANCE ALREADY WAS ROLLING TOWARD THE AC-CIDENT SCENE BY THE TIME SWIFT'S BATTERED CAR CAME OUT OF ITS THIRD ROLL.

CONCERN RAN HIGH...UNTIL DRIVER STAN

	SWIFT STEPPED FROM THE WRECKAGE...GAVE THE SIGN ALL WAS WELL...AND WALKED AWAY.
	IT'S ALL IN THE LIFE OF A RACE DRIVER. AND, WHAT A LIFE!
DJ & RP (BLACK)	OH YES! THE WINNER WAS NED BLACK, WHO WOUND UP SETTING A COUNTY FAIR GROUNDS TRACK RECORD THAT ALMOST WAS LOST IN THE EXCITEMENT OF A BAD ACCIDENT THAT TURNED OUT ALL RIGHT.

Thus, we have a complete package: an introduction, a voice-over film, and a tag or button, to round off the story. Let's say Dave Johnson's reading speed is a fairly standard five seconds for two of the half-lines. Computed that way, the introduction runs just about 15 seconds, the film is a loose 50 seconds of copy with a built-in pause to let the picture carry its own drama, and the tag is about 12 seconds more. The device of using a still picture (RP) of the Fair Grounds saves a little time, and since the focus of attention was the accident rather than the race, the time has been given over to the action, itself. Still for those interested in the race result, the package is rounded out by naming the winner and showing a still picture of him as a tag to the film.

When someone else has written the voice-over copy for the newscaster, he might, as suggested before, write in cue words to gear the newscaster for what scenes he must hit precisely and thereby provide a double check on the timing:

AUTO RACE FILM DJ-VO 1:00	THROUGH THE FIRST EIGHTY-FIVE LAPS IT WAS ROUTINE...ALMOST A DULL AFFAIR.
(SKID)	THEN, EVERYTHING CHANGED. DRIVER STAN SWIFT'S NUMBER THREE CAR GOT INTO TROUBLE.

	SWIFT COULDN'T STRAIGHTEN OUT...AND HE BROUGHT THE CROWD TO ITS
(BARRIER)	FEET AS HE HIT THE METAL AND CONCRETE WALL.
	FOR A WHILE, IT LOOKED BAD FOR THE POPULAR LOCAL DRIVER AS HIS CAR
(CAR TURNS OVER)	BOUNCED OFF THE BARRIER AND WENT INTO A SPEC-TACULAR SERIES OF ROLLS.
(ROLLS TWICE)	(PAUSE :07)
	THE OTHER SEVEN CARS HAD STOPPED AND THE AMBULANCE ALREADY WAS ROLLING TOWARD THE AC-CIDENT SCENE BY THE TIME SWIFT'S BATTERED CAR CAME OUT OF ITS THIRD ROLL.
(CROWD)	CONCERN. RAN HIGH...UNTIL DRIVER STAN
(OUT OF CAR)	SWIFT STEPPED FROM THE WRECKAGE...GAVE THE SIGN
(WAVE AND WALK)	ALL WAS WELL...AND WALKED AWAY.
	IT'S ALL IN THE LIFE OF A RACE DRIVER. AND, WHAT A LIFE!

Silent film or video tape often is used to set up a sound statement and occasionally is employed to bridge between two or more sound takes. Whichever the case, the newscaster or writer always must know exactly how much silent material there is and what it shows so a proper script can be prepared.

Quite another method of handling silent pictures is dealt with in a later chapter on reporting from the scene of a news story. One note of caution should be observed in writing voice-over copy. It is no help to the viewer to tell him just what it is he sees on film. Often, some imagination and effort are required to prepare a voice over script that enlarges on and enhances the picture. The effort is essential to proper use of the medium of television.

CHAPTER 10

TV Reporting Techniques

Established routes to the top positions in television news are few because the medium is so young. Most of the anchorman today, at both the network and local levels, were trained in newspapers, wire services or in radio. Whatever the background, when one enters the field of television news reporting, he or she is propelled into a totally new world of journalism. Whether the newcomer is cutting his teeth in network news or starting at the local station, there are certain technical aspects of film coverage that he must understand before venturing out on a story. Editorially, the only sure rule for the reporter to follow is that there are no hard and fast rules; he must understand that he's expected to make his way on the bases of his own industry, imagination and professional integrity.

While the primary consideration is and always must be the editorial content of the story, the television reporter must also concern himself with the pictorial possibilities of that story. He must take into account the logistical problems of getting a camera to the scene of the story. If he is out to make silent film, his problems are minimal. The 16-millimeter hand camera, or "Filmo," as it is known in the trade, is the most portable piece of equipment in the photographic repertory. It is spring wound and requires no outside power. Oftentimes, the local television reporter is expected either to know how to use a camera or be able to learn quickly so that he can cover stories as a combination newsman-cameraman.

It would seem that this might be an ideal situation if, indeed, young newsmen and women could handle the dual training of journalism and photography and put both elements together in practice. Under present and foreseeable conditions, however, both higher professional standards and union requirements ultimately would force the individual with the combined talents to choose between them and practice only one of them. At the network level, for instance, editorial demands are so exacting that a reporter's time is consumed with the day-to-day chores of gathering the facts of any event and putting them together in an accurate and interesting way. While he often helps his cameraman by suggesting certain pictorial material, he certainly would be more than overburdened by the need to double back after getting his story firmly in mind to do the actual filming of it. Then, too, it is rare for the networks to cover anything with silent film only, whereas it is the staple of many small television station's daily bill of fare.

The hand camera usually takes a 100-foot film load, or just about three minutes of pictures. In many local situations, that 100 feet of film might be the station's entire daily ration of newsfilm. The reporter might check into his office in the morning, look over the municipal schedule and the other events he knows are supposed to take place that day and plan his time in such a way that he can make a few feet of silent film of several events to use on that evening's local newscasts. Perhaps he will be furnished with an automobile with two-way radio by which someone can notify him while he's making his rounds if something newsworthy happens that would cause him to abandon his plan to cover the new story. Whatever his situation as far as budgetary and other restrictions are concerned, the newsman is expected to come back with something presentable. Perhaps his 100-foot roll of film has been spread over three or four events. The likelihood in this sort of operation is that the newsman will then have to process the film, edit it, write a script for it and perhaps even air it. Local television stations that operate this way demand a great deal for their money in the way of human effort.

SHOOTING SOUND FILM

While it is possible to cut many photographic corners with news coverage consisting only of silent film, the shooting of sound film is an entirely different proposition. Indeed, there are television stations that don't own sound cameras because they are so expensive, or else they restrict their use to the making of local commercials. Sometimes a persuasive news director will be able to prevail on management to spring the sound camera loose for some event of special interest in the community or perhaps get management to rent a sound rig for the occasion. The news director is indeed fortunate on these occasions if he is not pulled away from his primary assignment of covering the story to run the sound gear while a cameraman makes the film. This is, of course, a highly unsatisfactory arrangement for everyone concerned.

Good sound is enormously important in communicating. When sound is recorded properly on film, it is crisp and clear, readily understood. When it is not, it is muddy, crackly and hard to understand. Two different kinds of sound film are in general use today. The more primitive is optical sound, which is a system in which sound is recorded photographically on film. It is serviceable, but far from good. Much to be preferred and, naturally, more expensive is film that is striped with magnetic recording tape which produces high fidelity sound on film. Station film projectors must also be converted to use magnetic sound, but from the standpoint of a worthy end product, the cost is justified.

Beyond the consideration of equipment, however, is the even larger factor of manpower. There is no denying that news coverage on sound film requires certain expertise. The task of making good pictures should be left to a professional cameraman. An experienced soundman should handle the audio coverage and a newsman should be allowed to be a newsman; that is, unencumbered in his basic task of reporting the news.

When the television newsman goes to the scene of a news story to make any kind of sound film, his problems begin to multiply. Now, instead of the light, portable hand camera, he and his colleagues must work with a bulky sound camera. If they will be filming indoors, they must make certain there is a source of electrical power. Chances are, also they will need some kind of supplementary lighting. More and more today, newsfilm is shot in color, which poses additional problems of proper exposure. While some cameramen are physically strong enough to do a good job of shooting sound film with a hand-held camera, or one rigged into a shoulder pod, this is a difficult and often dangerous practice. Most cameramen aren't anxious to attempt this kind of filming, or leastwise not often.

In the field, then, the newsman must be concerned with a camera position and a solid footing for a tripod. In a news conference situation, for instance, there might be half-a-dozen or more cameras competing for the best position. In a crowd situation, the newsman often will find he must protect his cameraman and gear not only from the curious but sometimes also from the furious. He must set up in a convenient spot from which the story can be covered and where principals can be brought for interviews. The newsman and cameraman do retain the option of employing both the sound camera and a hand camera, using the latter to fill in with silent film those aspects of the story that cannot be reached with the sound rig. By the same token, it also is possible to use the sound camera to shoot silent film but, because of its weight and awkwardness, most cameramen prefer to use the hand camera wherever possible for silent film.

When the television newsman goes to the scene of a news story, he is concerned with filming a report that will represent the event fully and fairly. There are those events that can be anticipated, where something that is scheduled and where coverage can be planned in advance. When he goes to the scene of a breaking story, on the other hand, the newsman must realize that events already are in motion, and that he will have to use his news sense and ingenuity not just to catch up with but actually to get ahead of the event.

Basically, the television newsman has four primary methods of covering the news. First, there is the straightforward silent film report which amounts to taking the hand camera to the scene of an event and filming whatever seems pertinent. Secondly, he might be called upon to do a rounded film report, or "take-out," which might include several segments of sound on film, including an on-camera opening and closing, a narration and several interviews. This, obviously, is a much more extensive, complicated and time-consuming endeavor. The third basic method is an on-camera account of what has taken place or an analysis of a news event. Known as a "stand-upper," this system involves only the reporter, usually at the locale of a news event, talking into the camera with no action or other footage to support the presentation. The fourth basic item in the television newsman's repertory is the interview, and it is so important to frame and conduct interviews properly that the next chapter is devoted exclusively to the technique and the technical aspects of interviewing.

Given sufficient time (and he can't always count on that), the television reporter should be able to take full advantage of his medium for a reasonable blend of words and pictures that leaves the viewer with a basic understanding of what has taken place. Sometimes the events are elementary and easily understood, such as an accident of some kind. By and large, the newsman and his cameraman will arrive at the scene a fair time after the accident happened. Perhaps the injured are being removed or clean-up operations already are under way. Under those circumstances, all the newsman can do is to make some film of what remains of the event, itself, and what is taking place in its immediate aftermath. Where death and personal injury are involved, there are decided questions of good taste that the newsman must bear in mind, as well as making sure the principles are understood by the cameraman. The scene of suffering can be captured without invading the privacy of the victim and without graphic illustration of dismemberment or undue attention to human misery. When photographs of the dead or injured are essential to a story, they can be made on long shots, which convey the meaning of the event, instead of close-ups, which often make reality entirely too stark.

Just like any other good reporter, the television newsman will speak to police, fire and other officials at the scene to find out how much anyone knows at the time of the facts surrounding the event. He'll look also for eyewitnesses or possibly even participants who are able to tell what happened. When an individual has a particularly dramatic or informative story to tell, or an official seems to be able to characterize the event succinctly and well, the reporter probably will want to record that part of the story on film.

Primarily, the television reporter must set out with some idea in mind or be able to determine swiftly just how important the story is and how much time it is likely to merit on the air. Value judgments of the investment of time, energy and film to be made at the scene come only with experience. The instinct for judging the story properly will come quickly to those who apply themselves fully to their craft, by remembering procedures they follow in the field, equating them with film used on air, and learning by this kind of study where to cut corners and save time without sacrificing picture or editorial content. It is necessary to overshoot film in normal television reporting. There is no absolute way to judge a news event's development or, indeed, to "edit in the camera" so as to end up with precisely the amount of film that will go on the air. On the contrary, ratios of 15 or 20 feet of film shot for every foot used are common. Often in documentary shooting, where production values are higher and time is a lesser factor, ratios of film shot to film used will rise much higher, in the 50-to-one area. The networks view film stock as the least expensive cost they incur in news coverage and certainly would prefer the men in the field to overshoot and come home with good coverage than to miss a worthwhile shot just to hold film use down. For the local station, the film cost outlook might be rather different, although nobody in the news business wants to miss something dramatic or informative.

REPORTING THE PLANNED EVENT

Another example of the sort of story the reporter often is called upon to cover on film is an event that is arranged well in advance and for which coverage can be both anticipated and begun ahead of time. The announcement of a major municipal construction project is typical. Here, too, there must be some guideline of how much time will be given over to the story in the newscast on which the story eventually is used; of course, that remains a flexible factor. It might be, for instance, that elaborate architectural models of the new construction are available. The newsman might also be able to go to the existing site and make some silent film to be used for purposes of comparison in his final film package. Perhaps the mayor will announce the event, in which case the newsman should contact either him or an aide to find out if there will be an advance text of the speech available. If so, enormous savings of time and film can be made by reading through the speech ahead of time and marking off those portions that will definitely be used. The practice of issuing advance texts of speeches is common and a tremendous help in most cases to newsmen of all media and especially television reporters who might otherwise have to roll their cameras for 15 or 20 minutes or however long the speech runs, while knowing only a minute or so of the film has any chance of getting on air. On the other hand, the fact that an advance text has been distributed is no guarantee that the speaker won't have a last minute change of mind and alter it slightly, drastically or even throw it out entirely. The newsman equipped with an advanced text must follow it meticulously to look for changes that would make him look foolish if he missed them.

If it soon becomes apparent that the speaker is ad libbing a lot or departing widely from the text, the television newsman might have to roll his camera for self-protection, in which case he must note the changes on the advanced text or make notes of where the changes are. If the speaker delivers the speech as planned, the newsman who has marked it in advance for filming has the advantage of having perhaps one or two minutes of film to work with back at the studio, and that saves him time in screening all the film the entire speech would have consumed.

When the event takes place, the television reporter may have decided on a complete wrap-up that calls for an on-camera opening and closing. He can position himself at some representative spot at the event, film the opening and the narration with its leads into and out of the various elements in the film package and then do a close either in the same spot as the opening or another, related location. On the other hand, the newsman might even decide the model of the new construction would make a far more interesting opening shot than something from the ceremony. He might use some of the silent film he made in advance and do off-camera narration for the picture. It is entirely possible that he would elect to voice-over the entire package, never being seen, although it is far more traditional to locate the reporter at the scene of the event by showing him there sometime during an extensive take-out.

The key point is that a good newsman with a native or cultivated sense of picture and some imagination usually can put together interesting and informative packages of newsfilm. The photographic possibilities are limited only by his technical knowledge and the boundaries of his imagination. The more interested he is, the more he will learn about his medium and the more he will be able to do with it. Someone who either has an instinct for picture, or can develop it, surely will be able to find an interesting spot in television news. Then, too, there are enormous personal satisfactions to be drawn from putting together a complicated newsfilm package, seeing it spring to life on the screen, and knowing that your own good news judgment made it turn out well.

If there is one thing for the newsman to remember in making a filmed report, it is to make sure he gets enough silent film to illustrate his narration. The narration frequently is written at the scene of an event and recorded on film right there, or at a convenient place nearby. One practical problem the newsman must consider is that of selecting some spot where the background noise will be constant or, preferably, non-existent, unless it is pertinent to the story and is likely to be heard throughout the proper elements of the filmed report. This is a particular danger for reporters who work in the field and send their film back to the studio for someone else to edit. Of course, it is practical to wait if possible until all elements of a film take-out have been shot. Then, with everything firmly in mind, the reporter can write a more comprehensive narration which then can be put on film or recorded on tape or even telephoned in to news headquarters and recorded there for later matching with the film. Again, there are many possibilities for doing the job not just adequately, but doing it well.

ON-CAMERA OPENS AND CLOSES

Recording narration usually is a simple process. Since the reporter ordinarily is not seen during the narration, there is nothing to prevent him from reading his script as it is recorded, either on film or audio tape. In this case, the words are the important things. Indeed, many cameramen will shoot useless background while recording the narration on film. In such cases, it is more sensible to keep the camera on the reporter as he reads or to film something with some meaning just in the unfortunate case that the film breaks on the air. Cases of film breaking are rare, but they do happen, and when silent film is being played against narration in a double projector film piece, there's a 50-50 chance of salvaging the report on air. Double projection means that two film projectors, or film chains, are in operation. One usually shows the picture and the other carries the narration. In the unfortunate case of a break in the silent film, if the director has a usable picture on his track, or narration, he can go over to that projector and at least have something to put on air while the film editors in the projection room try to get the broken film restored and back on air. These are tense, desperate moments of patching and filling.

Much more troublesome to film are the on-camera portions of a filmed report, when the newsman should not just read a script, but instead should memorize at least enough of it to get his story started or finished. Many newsmen are glib enough to ad-lib an open or close. Others find they can remember better after writing something. The real tick in recording on-camera material, however, is not just remembering the thoughts but actually recalling the precise wording. Few reporters are so good all the time that they can always do their on-camera material right the first time and let it go at that. Indeed, standard practice, even with the best reporters, is to record the material at least twice to have one protection copy in case something is technically wrong with the original. It is no help in the cutting room to have two on-camera openings or closings that vary in editorial content or phrasing.

On-camera sections need not be long and almost anyone can commit 15 or 20 seconds' worth of copy to memory and retain it long enough to deliver it into a camera. Sometimes it will take a bit more doing than other times and the reporter having trouble is better off just to stop and start all over again. The best procedure in such cases is to stop fumbling, to pause for several seconds to allow a suitable break between sound sequences on film, slate the element and the take, and begin all over again. Slating means labeling what portion of the film is coming next as, for instance, the opening or the closing, an interview or the narration. The "take" is the number of times that particular portion has been done. If, for example, the reporter has flubbed three on-camera openings, he slates the next one as "Opening...Take Four." Everyone concerned, the reporter, cameraman, producers and film editors all hope he won't get into double take numbers, but if the reporter is having a particularly bad day, he is better off to take it again as many times as necessary to get it right. Another time he'll have a better day and get it in one or two takes.

Along with proper slating, it also is wise for the reporter to send a copy of his completed script along with the film. It saves time in note taking or preparing transcripts and indicates immediately to whoever is cutting the film what kind of package the reporter in the field has put together.

THE FACE-TO-CAMERA REPORT

Undoubtedly, the most difficult assignment the television reporter draws is covering the story with little or no picture possibility and having to recount the happening himself. Another possibility is that the news event is some complicated matter that cries out for explanation or even interpretation or analysis. In such cases, the reporter is faced not only with the basic news-gathering problems of getting his story, understanding it fully, and writing an account that will convey as much information as possible in as an informative way as he can, but he is confronted also with the ultimate problem of stepping in front of the camera to give his explanation. Here, too, he wants to be as informal as possible, to present his report in a conversational tone and to shun any suggestion of lecturing. Obviously, then, much depends on writing the script. The reporter making an on-camera presentation must have time to go over his material several times to get it down right and ready for delivery. Under normal circumstances, he would be expected to use between 45 seconds and perhaps one-minute-and-15 seconds for his report. Anything shorter than that almost precludes the possibility of getting any information across; anything more without accompanying picture can get somewhat boring unless it is a particularly vital story delivered in an engaging way.

For purposes of making the on-camera report, or stand-upper, it is acceptable for the reporter to hold the script in his hand and refer to it occasionally while putting the report on film. Unlike the brief on-camera opens and closes, reporters aren't usually expected to memorize lengthy, complicated pieces and, indeed, the occasional reference to the script lends authenticity to the stand-upper. Then, too, there is technical help available.

Visually, it is desirable to make one or more camera lens changes during any sort of on-camera report that goes beyond about 20 to 30 seconds. It could be that the cameraman elects to open on a wide shot of the reporter, especially if he has any kind of decent background in which to deliver the report.

Perhaps within ten to 15 seconds the cameraman should move into a medium close-up of the reporter. That might be an acceptable shot to hold for 20 to 30 seconds more. When it comes to the conclusion of the report and the sign-off, the cameraman probably would want to make that film on a close-up or even a tight close-up shot. If the reporter is having trouble remembering his copy or tends to get flustered after speaking directly to the camera for several paragraphs of copy, it is just as well for him to come to a complete halt after one or two paragraphs. At that point, he can take a break, re-read his next paragraph or two and let the cameraman reset his lens. As a matter of fact, for film editing purposes it is absolutely necessary to do this to avoid jump cuts or unnatural breaks in the picture. What the reporter must always remember to do, after any lens change, is to repeat exactly the last five or six words he said before stopping. This gives the film editors the chance to cut the lens change in smoothly, thus avoiding the obvious break or pause in the filming.

It is obvious that, for a pictorial medium like television, pictures are preferred to the straight on-camera news report. However, there are certain stories that simply do not lend themselves to photographic treatment, in which case the face-to-camera report must suffice.

VIDEO TAPE REPORTS

Almost everything that has been said about getting the story on film applies to video tape reports. For the local newsman, the question almost is academic because he will be confined to the use of film. Only the most news conscious local, independent stations will invest in mobile video tape equipment. One day, highly portable video tape gear will be generally available. For the moment, however, the news story to be reported directly on video tape must be within range of the electronic camera. For the present, video tape is more suited to a situation in which a subject involved in a news event can be brought to the studio to be interviewed there.

CHAPTER 11

The Interview

No single device is more important to the television newsman than the interview. Editorially, he must know how to find interesting interview subjects and then must be able to draw information from them in a way that improves his story. Basically, the newsman looks either for someone involved in a news story or for an expert who can shed light on a particular subject. Often, the ability to come up with good interviews makes the difference between routine and outstanding coverage.

In interviewing, as in all other facets of television journalism, the editorial function is bound up to a high degree by technical considerations. The use of film or video tape introduce a whole new set of factors for the reporter to deal with. Whether the television reporter is going into the field to get his story on film or will sit before an electronic camera in a studio, he must make every effort to be prepared for his subject. Obviously, it is impossible for a newsman to conduct an interview if he doesn't know what to ask the subject!

The situation is rather different on a breaking news story, for instance, when the newsman is sent in haste to the scene of some event and simply must feel his way, deciding on the basis of his observations who to interview and what to ask. The general and acceptable tendency always is to ask for a few more questions than necessary while the camera is running. There is always the tendency to let the interview run on too long, to the point that all spontaneity is gone and the subject matter is at least momentarily been exhausted. This is a question of news judgment and the answers essentially are drawn from experience. The reporter must be able to size up his story and his interview subject on the spot and to recognize whether or not he is getting useful information.

Still another vital consideration, and the actual basis for the immediate decision confronting the reporter, is the need for close attention to what is being said by his subject. Inexperienced reporters often are preoccupied with their overall story, or else they may lose track of what the subject is saying while framing another question. The great danger here is that by not listening intently, the reporter may miss something important and not follow it up. It also is discourteous to ask someone for an interview and then fail to pay attention.

It is acceptable, and in some cases even desirable, for a reporter to approach an interview with key questions written down. If the subject and the interviewer are seated opposite one another, it is a simple matter for the reporter to conceal his notes in his lap. If they are standing, perhaps he can learn to refer quickly and unobtrusively to the notes when the camera is on the subject and then keep them out of sight when actually asking his questions. For his own development, however, the reporter should try to limit his reliance on notes and to cultivate his memory.

Another reason the reporter should pay strict attention to what the interview subject is saying is to determine whether or not the subject is responding to his line of questioning. Even if the newsman has done his homework well, it gains him little to allow the subject to ramble on into unrelated material or, worse yet, just a spate of generalities.

There is little to be gained for the reporter to approach an interview subject with the air of the grand inquisitor. Rather, he should be courteously firm and must remain in control of his interview to make certain he gets the best information he can on the story he is after. The reason a newsman interviews anyone is to find out what the individual knows or thinks about a subject, and basic human differences are a factor in news coverage. One person will run on like the river; another must have the answers pried out of him. Both situations require judgment and decision. Generally, the newsfilm interview needn't be long.

On a breaking story, it ordinarily is wiser to interview several eyewitnesses or participants if they are available. If they have something worthwhile to say, stay with them for a while, perhaps from three to five minutes of filming. If not, wrap the interview up gracefully and move along.

In the case of an exploratory report or extensive film "take out," it often is necessary to devote more time to interviews with experts. Here, the newsman begins from quite a different premise than he does with the breaking story and eyewitness account. In the case of an expert, the subject has been selected in advance. The newsman must proceed on the assumption that he knows his subject. Some experts are spellbinders, easily able to articulate their subject matter; others, again, obviously are more suited to the written word and perhaps camera shy. The difficulty the newsman faces with the spellbinder is finding a logical point to cut off the interview. If, for instance, the interview has proceeded smoothly for 15 or 20 minutes, the reporter will long since have sensed he is getting much more than he can use. Unless the subject is addressing himself in deep detail to one point, the reporter may see an opportunity for several, separate uses of the interview. Otherwise, the newsman must control the situation and bring the interview to a conclusion when he has the information he set out to get.

Most television news departments maintain some sort of newsfilm library in which both used and unused film and video tape are stored for as long as anyone in charge thinks the material might have some value. The obvious key to an effective newsfilm library is an accurate filing system in which members of the organization know how to find what they need in a hurry. Many news stories tend to repeat themselves in greater or lesser detail and an up-to-date library often will give a station a great edge because filmed or taped material to illustrate that story is readily accessible. When a reporter has produced a particularly effective interview, it is wise for him to make brief notes on the subjects on which he thinks future use might be made.

QUESTIONS THAT ARE QUESTIONS

When time allows, many interviewers like to spend a few minutes getting acquainted with the individual to be interviewed. This is especially true in cases where an extended interview can be anticipated and the subject is expected to cover a lot of information. This practice is beneficial if it really does get the preliminaries out of the way before the camera starts to roll. It often is helpful to discuss in general terms what the reporter is after and the general line of questioning he expects to take. On the other hand, it is unwise, actually, to go over the questions in advance because of the danger of robbing the actual interview of spontaneity.

Perhaps the most common failing of inexperienced television reporters, especially, is the tendency to ask questions that sound more like answers. Generally, this indicates the reporter has either not thought out what he wants to ask or else has lost control of the situation. Whenever possible, questions should be short and direct. Specific questions are more likely to bring specific answers. Long, rambling, disjointed questions are likely to confuse interview subjects and, when they actually do make it through the cutting room and onto the air, they only confuse the viewer.

When the interview subject does tend to stray, the interviewer must pose questions that will get him back on the track and keep him there. Often this can be accomplished by trying to pin the subject down on a specific point. The important thing to remember is that the value of any interview is directly proportional to the information it develops about the intended subject.

THE INTERVIEW SETTING

The physical surroundings in which an interview is conducted ordinarily are determined by its locale. In a studio setting, the interviewer and subject can face each other across a table or sit alongside each other on a sofa or in easy chairs. If a table is used, a single microphone can be set between them or a boom microphone could be suspended over them and out of range of the camera. In the more informal sofa setting, use of the boom mike also is possible, or else the interviewer and subject can use, suspended from the neck, a lavalier microphone; and both are free to address each other in a conversational, living room sort of setting.

In the field or out on a breaking story, the situation is quite different. Cordless microphones are used rarely in hard news coverage or in news feature filming. Much more common is the situation in which the reporter must hold a microphone that is connected directly to the sound rig. The newsman must be able either to get the subject in front of the camera or the camera in front of the subject, and this, in turn, poses the problem of finding a strategic location for the interview. Then, when the interview finally is in progress, the newsman must pass the microphone back and forth between the subject and himself. Occasionally, a situation will develop in which the reporter might have more than one interview subject at the same time and he must wield the microphone for the entire group. Whichever the case, the mike should be moved as little as possible so that it does not become a distraction both for the subject and the viewer. It is a necessary but awkward appurtenance to soundfilm operations and should be made inconspicuous as possible.

An even greater problem for the television newsman is the mass interview situation in which he has to scramble against his competition to get a story on film. Airport arrivals present the most common example of this kind of coverage in which, for instance, a celebrity or public figure is coming to town. Local newsmen and perhaps reporters from out of town may converge with their cameras to film the arrival of the distinguished visitor and perhaps to get in a few quick questions on the spot. Everyone has seen film of mob scenes in which a reporter is trying to reach over other pushing, shoving, anxious newsmen in an effort to get a microphone into a spot where it will even pick up the words spoken by the harried visitor. Often, too, these situations get so far out of hand that even if the reporter is lucky enough to record some sound, there is no guarantee the cameraman will be able to get a usable picture of anything but the shoving match. Much to be preferred is the general news conference. When an important person comes to town and can't afford the time for several individual interviews, newsmen should get together to try to arrange a news conference in which all reporters from all media have equal access to the guest and equal opportunity to pose questions. This hardly qualifies as a true interview situation, but it often provides the only alternative.

If a public information officer or press agent handles the news conference arrangements, it is up to him to make certain everybody gets a chance to cover the story properly. Otherwise, local newsmen should be able to work out their own cooperative arrangement. Normally, once his camera is in place, the newsman can operate on the premise that his camera will roll throughout the proceedings, and he can concentrate on the subject matter and get his own chance to ask questions. He should, however, be aware of how much film his cameraman has and know when he has to stop filming to reload if that situation arises. It would be wasteful of time and energy to have the newsman spouting a series of questions at a time when his own camera is not running.

ESTABLISHING SHOTS

A fundamental consideration in filming or video taping an interview is to provide all the technical help needed by those who in the end will edit that film or tape. Step number one in any recorded interview is the establishing shot. As the name indicates, the establishing shot is a picture that introduces a segment of a news story and provides the background for the spoken introduction. In the case of a straight filmed or taped interview, it often is desirable to put the picture of the subject on the screen before he begins to speak so that perhaps some of his credentials can be presented and his relation to the story explained. To make this possible, the cameraman might run off a few feet of film of the subject. If his expertise grows out of a function he performs, such as an athlete, it might be well to show him doing that for which he is well-known. Again, if the expert is a doctor who has performed some kind of research experiment, it might be well to picture him in his laboratory, especially if the interview actually was conducted there. In the case of a purely intellectual discussion, just as establishing shot of the face of the subject in close up or just sitting with the interviewer might do.

With this film or tape available, the newsman producing the report can decide that he needs five, ten or however many seconds of silent establishing film to get smoothly into the interview. Establishing shots are even more important in those frequent instances when the interview is to be cut into a filmed package and it would look ridiculous' to set the interview up with another picture that doesn't actually relate to the interview. Ordinarily, establishing shots are made with silent film specifically for a voice over treatment. In cases where no silent film or tape was made, it is possible to use the picture of the subject speaking and hold the track under or out entirely. The subject's lips will be moving but this is a fallback method of introducing a subject over a picture of himself. Still another possible way to introduce a speaker on film or tape, when it is either inconvenient or impossible to do it with a proper voice-over, is to have the art department make up a superimposure (super) with the speaker's name and a word or two of identification, which can be flashed on the screen as the subject begins his speech. It also is wise to use this kind of super in cases of long sound takes to remind viewers of the identity of the speaker.

CUTAWAY SHOTS

The primary goal of editing filmed and video taped interviews is to wind up with a product in which edits cannot be detected by the home viewer; that is to say the selected segments are connected neatly and naturally and fall right into place. This is accomplished mainly by making pictures of scenes or individuals associated with the interview.

If you will think back, you'll probably be able to recall many instances in which you've seen a speaker on television come to a point at which his words continue but the scene changes so that the speaker is no longer seen but rather the picture becomes that of the audience, perhaps, or a cameraman working his rig. Audiences and other photographers are the most common cutaways because they're usually available. Whatever the scene, the cutaway is absolutely vital to successful film and tape editing.

The purpose of the cutaway is the avoid the "jump cut." Often it is possible to take a straight run of film from an in-

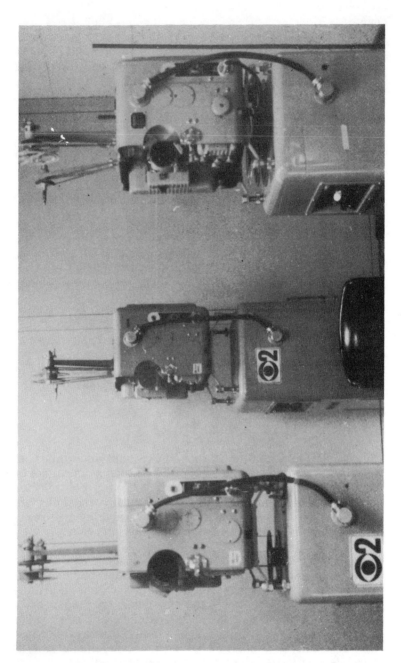

Sixteen millimeter projectors arranged for screening a triple projector film piece. (Courtesy Norman Goldman)

terview. This poses no problem. It is good fortune, indeed, to find a 45-second or one-minute take that is so entirely responsive to the situation that it simply can be lifted from the original and run on the air or included in a film or tape package. Problems arise in those common situations where it either is necessary or desirable to shorten the speaker's remarks or to join parts of several sections of a speech or interview while keeping everything in proper context. Because of the way sound projectors are designed, the sound runs ahead of the picture on film. In the case of optical sound film, the sound is advanced by 26 frames so that the picture passing the lens corresponds with the sound reproduced by the sound head, which is located below the lens. In the case of magnetic sound film, the sound is advanced by 28 frames. In both cases, the difference translates into a matter of just a bit over one second. Because of this variance, it is necessary to splice a cutaway shot of either 26 or 28 frames into a single projector sound cut at a point where the speaker has ended a sentence or permitted his voice to drop off enough to make it sound as if he has completed a sentence. To rejoin sound to sound in this situation, it is necessary to pick up at the beginning of a sentence or else, because of the advanced sound track, the picture will briefly show the subject with his lips moving and no sound coming forth. At the very beginning of a single projector sound take, it is possible to get into the take in the middle of a sentence by warning the director of the way the film is cut and having him wait a second or so longer than he would normally to take the film, or until the lip flap has passed. In an interior single projector cut, however, there is no such way to avoid the lip flap, so the problem must be avoided by cutting at the start of a sentence.

Far more flexibility can be found in cutting sound film in the double projector manner in which cutaway shots either in silent or sound film are put on a second reel on a second projector. The film editor who prepares the double projector film package spaces the cutaways precisely with blank film in order that when the director hears the cue signalling the cut in the sound, he calls in the second projector picture or picture and sound and holds on that until the new sound cut he wants on the other reel comes up ready to be put on air. A typical sound cutaway is audience applause. Care must be exercised in using applause, however, because it is entirely improper to insert applause at a point in which the audience did not in fact react. If the edit is to be made where the audience did applaud then the shot is in order. Otherwise, a cutaway of the audience listening or perhaps a shot of other speakers at the head table or on the stage will do just as well. It is not for news personnel cutting the film to editorialize by selecting convenient spots for applause.

In the case of video tape, the problem of advanced sound track is not so critical, because the sound is nearer the picture. It is just as necessary, however, to avoid jump cuts by the same judicious use of cutaway shots to keep the pictorial action flowing naturally. In this regard, it might be noted that cutaways come in handy not only for cutting sound on film but also for obviating pictorial problems as well. It is a common trait of public figures who wear eyeglasses, for instance, to use them for emphasis or dramatic effect while delivering a speech. Perhaps the speaker has his glasses on during one passage, then takes the glasses off, gestures with them or simply puts them on the rostrum at another time. It would look ridiculous, of course, to run a film clip in which a sound cut has been made showing the speaker with glasses on in one instant and then to show him without glasses a few seconds later with no kind of transition in between. There would also be an obvious jump or break in the film as the splice flashes through the projector and onto the picture tube and then a laughable juxtaposition of bespectacled speaker to unbespectacled speaker.

REVERSE QUESTIONS AND LISTENING SHOTS

In an interview situation, the cameraman does not usually have an audience or other cameramen to fall back on for necessary cutaway shots. His recourse, then, is to use the reporter, himself. Ordinarily, after the cameraman has made his establishing shots of the interview subject alone and with the reporter, he zooms in on the subject. Most interviews are filmed entirely with the camera on a close-up or medium close-up shot of the subject. After the interview, the cameraman must make film of the reporter in a listening attitude. Just as the crowd shot or other cameramen serve for cutting purposes, so does the reporter sitting there looking alert and interested. This close-up picture of the newsman sometimes is referred to as a "reaction shot," but that really is a misnomer in that newsmen are not supposed to react to the remarks of an interview subject or anyone else in any way that could be taken to connote either approval of or disagreement with what the speaker is saying. It is permissible for the reporter to nod slightly to indicate understanding. To do more than that, facially or verbally, might be construed as editorial or something it should not be.

One other helpful practice in any interview situation is for the cameraman to shoot the reporter's questions over again, separately. In the original interview, the camera will be focussed on the subject. The reporter's questions will be heard, but he will not usually be seen delivering them. When the interview is over, the cameraman reverses the position of his camera so as to be able to focus on the reporter while keeping him in what was his proper relation to the subject. Then, with the camera on a close-up or medium close-up, the reporter repeats at least the key questions he asked, and preferably all of them and, again, he must make every effort to phrase the questions as they were phrased originally. The purpose of this is that in editing the film, the reverse question can be cut in to shorten other answers and thus keep the picture flowing naturally in the nature of any other kind of cutaway shot. Since it is so important for reverse questions to match the originals, perhaps for the novice interviewer it would be best to write down in advance what he intends to ask and to jot down the other questions he does ask as the interview materializes in order to repeat them with precision. This process sometimes can be simplified if someone in the film crew or even an interested bystander can be prevailed upon to make note of the questions. When a field producer is on hand, the unit doing the interview can save the production team a lot of extra work simply by listing the reverse questions and supplying some editorial notes on the points on which the subject responded well or are particularly pertinent to the story. For the local reporter working under manpower restrictions, it's just one more job he must handle on his own, but he can make the work easier for himself and his film editors and colleagues by paying strict attention to questions, answers, reverse questions and cutaways, whether he is conducting an interview on film or video tape.

THE LIVE INTERVIEW

Editorially, everything recommended in this chapter for the filmed and video taped interview holds true for the live interview. Proper preparation for the live interview is perhaps even more necessary because, as the name indicates, a live interview is done on the air and there is no leeway for slip-ups or slipshod work. If the subject of an interview is the author of a book, as so often is the case, it is common courtesy for the interviewer to read the book entirely if possible or at least familiarize himself with its contents and key sections. There is great concern within the field of broadcast journalism due to the effort to use television simply for the purposes of promoting the sale of a book or other product. Here, again, utmost care is called for in selecting interview subjects with obvious commercial interests. It is fair to give an author credit for his book, but it is also essential for the newsman to frame his interview and control his interview in such a way that it provides worthwhile information and not just a plug for the book or product involved.

CHAPTER 12

Film & Video Tape Editing

Even when the television reporter has his story on film, his work is not over. Whether it is silent coverage, a lengthy take-out or an interview, he is responsible for getting the film to wherever it will be processed. Many well-equipped television stations insist on controlling the processing of film and are willing to make the substantial investments involved. The best, most modern color film processing machines now available cost from about $20,000 for a small model capable of processing about 33 feet of color film per minute to the enormous, room-sized processors that handle 56 feet per minute and cost as much as $60,000. Black-and-white processing machines are somewhat less expensive. They are capable of processing either silent or sound film at an average rate of about 60 feet per minute. It must be considered, too, that such equipment requires trained personnel to use and service it properly and to prepare and maintain the correct chemical solutions for the best, most economical use. Of course, it is possible for television stations to purchase secondhand equipment, and all too often there is the tendency to use equipment such as a film processor until it literally is worn out. Newsmen and other manpower in small television stations are called upon often to achieve some almost unbelievable feats to keep ancient, tired equipment from chewing raw film into celluloid scraps and ruining a day's run of newsfilm. Often in these situations, the economy is difficult to see.

When a television station does not own its own film processing equipment, it must arrange with a nearby commercial laboratory to do the work. This always is a problem in that it establishes a way station in a high-speed, high-pressure business which needs corners cut rather than expanded. The other obvious disadvantage in dealing with an outside lab is that it must service other customers and priority conflicts can arise. Unless the television station can be guaranteed that its often considerable needs can be met, there is nothing to be gained in using any given laboratory.

Whichever arrangement the station uses, the newsman must take processing time into consideration when he is filming a story. If he is shooting for use that day, which is more than likely in most cases, it gains him nothing to capture a story in the camera and have it miss air because the film didn't get to the developer in time.

FILM STOCK

Still another technical factor in the myriad of detail the television newsman must understand is the film stock on which the story is shot. When black-and-white film was used exclusively, the networks relied mostly on a film stock that processed to a negative, while local stations still rely mainly on reversal film that produces a positive print directly and skips the negative stage. Generally, this is cheaper and more convenient for the local station. The networks, on the other hand, preferred the negative processing because of the infinitely greater quality it gives. Negative film can be run on the air simply by reversing the polarity of the projector, which is a simple, flip-of-the-switch kind of operation. The other advantage the networks derived from the use of black-and-white negative is that it reproduces well. Newsfilm syndication and other film sales are a source of income for the networks, and with negative, high-quality prints they are readily available.

In the case of reversal film, the situation is complicated in that prints cannot be made from the original positive print. Instead, a duplicate negative must be made, and the prints struck from that negative, with a substantial drop-off in quality. One other consideration is that it is more of a problem to screen negative film because the viewer who is choosing the shots must be able to make the mental flip of the polarity switch and recognize that what he is looking at in the screening room is the exact opposite of what will be seen on air; that is, the blacks will be white and the whites will be black.

Color newsfilm has changed things substantially. In color, reversal stock is altogether satisfactory from the quality standpoint and preferable in that negative processing with color is too slow normally for news operations. It is possible to make good prints from the reversal positive, and a screening of the positive print gives the newsmen and film editors the great advantage of seeing for themselves exactly what they will be putting on the air exactly as it will appear.

Since the late 1960s, color film has been used almost exclusively in network news operations. The networks put black-

and-white film on the air only in extraordinary circumstances, such as those cases in which an affiliate or free-lancer has come up with spectacular footage. For the film crews at the source of a film story, color does create additional problems of lighting, but, when the first color television set was sold, a new era of television news was begun, and eventually even local stations will be forced by competition to give up the old ways of black-and-white to go to the better, if more costly, color film coverage.

GETTING FILM READY FOR THE AIR

Once the newsfilm has been processed and delivered to the newsman who will handle it or the editorial team that will decide its ultimate usage, several vital steps must be taken. Under normal conditions, it is imperative that all newsfilm be put on a projector and screened for quality and content. Photography, as any dabbler in the art knows, is full of potential dangers. Among the most common problems that can arise even when a full-time, professional cameraman is on the job are: exposure difficulties that occur rather more frequently with color than with black-and-white film and occasionally even when a competent man is behind the lens; scratches on film as a result of a problem either in the camera or in the developing process; or off-speed sound film that distorts the sound quality to the point where it is not usable often the result of sub-freezing cold in which the camera cannot reach proper running speed. Off-speed film often can be counteracted by the use of a variable speed projector, which usually is available, however, only in network operations. In the case of scratched film, a decision must be made quickly as to whether the story can be cut around the scratches if they are intermittent or whether the story, itself, is good enough to air even with the defect in the film, which can be annoying to the viewer but often is more of a problem for production-oriented people who sometimes give more weight to film quality than to news content. This, ultimately, is the decision that must be made when any kind of film defect does turn up. It is one of the many purely subjective conclusions newsmen must draw on the basis of experience and desire to perform the various tasks well.

The actual screening process can be brief or time consuming, depending entirely on the amount of film that must be viewed. It takes one minute to look at 36 feet of 16-millimeter film or roughly three minutes per 100 feet of film. Obviously, then, it takes about half and hour to look at 1,000 feet, etc. The newsman who was on hand when the story was filmed should have a pretty good idea of what the film contains. If he doesn't, he wasn't paying proper attention. If he has the ultimate responsibility of cutting the film into an airworthy package, he has the decided advantage of knowing where to look for what. It often is helpful for the reporter to make notes so that he can tell which segment of film is on which roll if a time crisis does arise. At any rate, by the time he has finished shooting his story, he should have a clear idea in mind of what he will use in his finished cut.

In cases where film is sent in to news headquarters and someone else must start from the beginning, the situation obviously is quite different. Certainly the reporter in the field will send in instructions or at least some advice on where to locate various segments on the film. His script serves as a basic framework for the cut. Still, someone picking up at that point should have the opportunity to look at all the film because to him falls the ultimate responsibility of producing an airworthy product. One helpful technique in wading through great amounts of film, and especially in screening lengthy interviews, is to run a stopwatch on the film, starting it from zero at the head of each reel, and making notes regarding what takes place at what time on each separate reel. Later, in the actual cutting process, any adept film editor can convert minutes and seconds into feet of film and go quickly to the portion the newsman wants. Still another helpful technique is that of "flagging" the film. What this means, simply, is that when a newsman and film editor sit down in a screening room to view large amounts of film, the editor should tear a sheet of paper into thin strips. When the newsman either sees or hears something he thinks he will want to use, he should ask the film editor to insert a piece of paper, or "flag," at that point in the reel. It will stick there as a marker for the editor to roll down to with no undue loss of time. Here, too, it is necessary for the newsman to keep his flags straight so that by making notes he will know what each flag represents.

When all the available film has been screened, the newsman ordinarily must make up his mind in a hurry how he is going to put the package together. It could be that he will decide to cut it in a way that is entirely different from that envisioned by the reporter at the scene. More often, though he will use the framework decided upon by the man who covered the story and then use his own discretion when it comes to selecting portions of interviews called for within the package. Then, too, in situations where a piece produced in the field is to be cut by someone else, the person directly involved with a newscast is more likely to know the time requirements that must be met. Perhaps the field reporter built a film package he expected to run for four, five or even six minutes. By the time the film arrived at news headquarters, the producer assigned to cut it has been told that he must hold it to a maximum of, say, two and a half minutes. Obviously, something the field reporter wanted to include is going to have to fall by the wayside. The producer must know what is in the film in order to make a valid judgment of what must stay and what can safely go.

There are certain production shortcuts that can be taken when a newsman finds himself in a time bind, as so often he does. Perhaps an unexpected delay has occurred in shipment or processing. Now, instead of the three hours he expected to have to put his film package together, he finds he has less than an hour. If, for instance, he has 1,000 feet of film to cope with, he knows immediately that there just will not be enough time to screen it entirely and then cut it properly. The best that can. be made of this kind of dilemma is to screen the silent material on a viewer, which means that the silent film is separated from the sound film and run through a 16-millimeter viewer. Instead of grinding through a projector at 36 feet per minute, the film editor can whip the film through the viewer at a much faster rate. There is no comparison between the two methods in terms of proper screening because the picture area of a viewer is about two inches square or a bit better, whereas a regular 16-millimeter picture screen is large enough to bring out all the detail in the film. In emergencies, however, sacrifices must be made and the newsman and film editor at least will have some idea of the silent picture they have to work with.

In the case of sound film, the editor can run the film through a sound reader, or "squawk box" as it is called, and then through the viewer so that the film editor and newsman can hear what is said on the sound track and see the corresponding picture. Again, this is far from the ideal way to edit film, but sometimes it is all that time will allow.

When the newsman and film editor are set to put the film package together, it is absolutely necessary for the newsman to give his film editor precise, explicit instructions. Where sound takes are involved, the newsman should prepare specific notes which give the film editor exact in cues and out cues, or else he must be able to pick out his sound takes quickly on the sound reader. The film editor first pulls all his shots, or separates the usable material from the unusable or

View of a typical film editor's bench. The film is running through a synchronizer. Notice the 16-mm viewer in the background. (Courtesy Norman Goldman)

"out-takes," as they are called. Normal practice is for the editor to hang the separate pieces of usable film in a barrel or container with numbered pins or, if not numbered, hang them from left to right or right to left in an order in which he can identify each chip as he splices the shots into the finished air reel. The great advantage of working with film is that an adept editor can make an edit, or splice, in a matter of seconds. Editors who are not only adept but also are imaginative and interested can make a tremendous difference in the end product, often lending pictorial assistance to a newsman who's

Pieces of film are hung over a "barrel" until the editor is ready to splice them together. (Courtesy Norman Goldman)

primary concern is editorial content. Often, there are situations where the two interests can blend to make a vastly superior film package. Here again it boils down to a matter of constructive cooperation.

In the small television station, the procedure often is quite different. Indeed, it too often is true that the harried newsman who does everything even is expected to do the physical splicing of film because there is no one else to do it at the time. Unquestionably, it is another fine technical asset to be able to splice film, but few individuals are so well rounded that they can make film, edit it, write news copy and broadcast it all with equal facility. Happily, as the newsman advances up the television news ladder, more demands are placed upon his strong points and specialties and no longer is he expected to be a jack-of-all-television-news trades.

VIDEO TAPE

Video tape, as has been mentioned, opened up an entirely new area of television and gave broad new flexibility to news operations, but initially there were some problems. In the early days of video tape, it had to be spliced manually and it usually took technicians with deft hands and alert minds to do it well. It was almost impossible, except in cases of pure luck, to make a tape splice in less than 20 minutes. Newsmen accustomed to working with film found it frustrating to stand around helplessly waiting for a single splice during a period in which they knew literally hundreds of film splices could have been made. Often, it boiled down to a matter of being able to select a straight run of video tape with no edits, or else that editorial and pictorial source was cut off in news operations. In the late 1960s, color video tape evolved. The original low-band color quickly gave way to high-band color, which results in much higher quality and reproduces so readily. Often in news work it is necessary to make copies, or "dubs," of video tape. With low-band color, it was possible to make one copy and then one copy of that copy. After the "second generation," however, the quality drop-off was beyond normal standards of usability. With high-band color, however, it is possible to go to as many as five generations before the quality problem arises.

Tape Editing

Unlike film, the editing of video tape is a complicated matter. Video tape made in the United States is recorded at a standard 525 lines. Tape recorded in Europe, for instance, has

625 lines. To be used here, it must be converted to 525 lines. Tape recorded on one video tape machine often is sent to another station for editing on another machine and sometimes doesn't match easily. Video tape contains electrical impulses, or edit pulses, that must be matched at a splice in order to prevent picture "break-up" on the air, a situation in which the taped picture scrambles momentarily. Even today, most conscientious video tape editors try to allow about 15 minutes for a manual splice.

Here, too, technological advances are rapid. By the end of the 1960s, processes were in use by which video tape splices could be made almost automatically and that tremendous time gap was closed. With these developments, the manual splicing of tape was largely eliminated and electronic splicing was developed. The new processes are in widespread use in network operations and in commercial television production, but the equipment is expensive and it will be long years before it is in general use in television stations across the country. Indeed, this is another area in which the difference between the network and local ways of doing things is almost unbelievable. Video tape equipment, to begin with, is costly to buy, to install and to maintain properly. The recording tape, itself, is expensive and small stations often try to reuse tape too often. Tape does have a tendency to shed or to flake if it is played too often or is erased and reused again and again. When this happens on the air, the picture is lost at least momentarily. The networks keep close tabs on tape use and discard it rather than risk any problems on air.

Today, it is common practice in network operations to transfer as much newsfilm as possible to video tape before broadcast. This is especially necessary when the film package is a complicated double projector piece, or perhaps even a triple projector production. This is another example of network precaution. It is far simpler to roll a piece of tape into a newscast than to hit a complicated piece of film and have it come out exactly right on the air when the pressures are at their highest.

Aside from the technical considerations of editing video tape, the production techniques are much the same as in film editing. If the newsroom is equipped with a closed circuit or internal monitor system, it is possible to view video tape in the news area. Otherwise, it must screened right on the video tape machine. As with film, a newsman must make a rundown of what happens at what time on the tape, or else take his timings from the tape machine's footage counter. He uses cutaway shots in the same manner as he does with film and strives always for the most felicitous balance of pictorial and editorial quality.

While some newsmen do, either of necessity or desire, develop an ability to splice film, it is highly unlikely for one to include the physical editing of video tape in his storehouse of talents. At any rate, he shouldn't have to.

CHAPTER 13

The Completed Script

Probably the most practical way to illustrate most of the elements of the television newscast, discussed in foregoing chapters, is to put them together within the framework of a finished script. Since a format for a half-hour network newscast already is presented in Chapter 8, it seems sensible to flesh that format out and make it do more work. The following material is fictitious, but, real or imagined, it will serve to demonstrate one basic approach to television news and one way to use some of the tools of television.

For purposes of illustration, every word to be heard on the air appears in the script. Normal material also is presented as it would appear in the script; that is, in the right-hand or audio column. Transcripts of actuality material or interviews also are included. When it comes to film take-outs, they, too, are presented in the standard split-page manner, with at least some attempt to indicate what sort of picture would be seen with the narration in point.

Again, a reminder that each separate element within the newscast carries its own number, and individual items within those numbered sections carry a separate letter for ease of organizing the script. It is too easy to create on-the-air problems with improperly marked or collated scripts. When it becomes necessary to substitute or "sub," an item, the substitution should carry some designation to let everyone know it, such as the marking NEW 3B, or SUB 3B, etc. Again, it doesn't matter what the designation is as long as it is understood clearly by everyone.

In this make believe newscast script, two half-lines are calculated to consume five seconds so that they conform to the allotted times in the format. It is permissible, of course, to shift the formatted times around as needed, provided the times stay within original limitations. Speeches and interview material in the examples are approximated, again for purposes of saving space and the author's "creative" labor pains. Explanatory notes here have been kept to a minimum.

1. OPEN & ANNOUNCE S.O.F. ON 16-4 (S.O.F. In this case it would be musical background sound...with copy read by a staff announcer.)	(MUSIC...UP FULL FOR :05, THEN UNDER) THIS IS THE X.Y.Z. EVENING NEWS...A ROUND-UP OF LATE DEVELOPMENTS FROM ACROSS THE NATION AND AROUND THE WORLD...GATHERED AND PREPARED BY THE IN-TERNATIONAL NEWS ORGANIZATION OF THE X.Y.Z. TELEVISION NETWORK.
SUPER (DATE)	TODAY IS WEDNESDAY, OCTOBER TENTH...AND THERE'S NEWS THIS DAY OF A MAJOR INTERNATIONAL AGREEMENT... A PRESIDENTIAL JOUR-NEY... OF A BREAK-THROUGH IN AIR SAFETY... AND AN IMPROMPTU ROCK CONCERT IN PITTS-BURGH. THE DETAILS ON ALL THE NEWS NOW FROM DAVE JOHNSON:
2. DJ & RP (DRAWING OF BROKEN WEAPONS)	GOOD EVENING. THE SENATE SAID YES TODAY TO A NEW VENTURE IN DISARMAMENT...AND THE MOVE PROMPTED A QUICK PRESIDENTIAL TRIP. LATE THIS AFTERNOON, THE SENATE CLOSED OUT A LENGTHY AND OFTEN HEATED DEBATE AND VOTED, EIGHTY-SEVEN TO

164

RP (SENATE VOTE)	TWELVE, TO APPROVE A TREATY COMMITTING THE UNITED STATES TO JOIN THE OTHER SUPERPOWERS IN A SHARP CUTBACK IN ARMS PRODUCTION.
	THE VOTE WAS SUB-STANTIALLY MORE THAN THE TWO-THIRDS REQUIRED FOR PASSAGE.
(MAP: RP EUROPE)	WITHIN MINUTES OF THE SENATE DECISION, PRESIDENT MITCHELL AN-NOUNCED HE WILL LEAVE TOMORROW ON A QUICK TOUR OF FIVE EUROPEAN CAPITALS.
POP ON (ROUTE)	THE JOURNEY WILL TAKE HIM FROM WASHINGTON TO LONDON, BRUSSELS, PARIS, BONN AND ROME.
	THERE WAS NO MISTAKING THE ELATION IN THE PRESIDENT'S WORDS:

3. PRESIDENT MITCHELL
    VT - 8
    RUNS 2:15
	IN CUE: A piller of my candidacy...

(TRANSCRIPT)

was the promise to move the United States forward into a new era of world peace. I do honestly feel that a vital step in that direction was taken this afternoon by the Senate. My deepest thanks go to the statesmen on both sides of the aisle who worked so hard for so long to rally the necessary votes and a goodly number beyond that.

I do appreciate some of the hesitancy in our country, and I can only ask for the faith and trust of those still unsure. Every conceivable safeguard of this country's interest has been considered. My advisers and I have assured and reassured ourselves that this is the right moment. That an international climate now exists to take this giant step together.

Having thus sought to assure my countrymen, I will leave tomorrow morning to deliver similar assurances, in person, to our allies in Western Europe. Their support of the drive for disarmament never flagged. They know far better than we the ravages of war. Their fears were our fears. But, beginning tomorrow, I shall be able to report optimistically to the Prime Minister of Britain, the President of Belgium, the Premier of France, the Chancellor of West Germany and the President of Italy. This is my third trip to Europe.

OUT CUE: IT IS THE ONE I LOOK FORWARD TO THE MOST, THANK YOU.

4. DJ

AN OBVIOUSLY PLEASED PRESIDENT MITCHELL.
DOMESTICALLY, HOWEVER, THE PRESIDENT MUST SETTLE A BATTLE WITHIN HIS OWN OFFICIAL FAMILY OVER HOW MUCH MONEY THE GOVERNMENT CAN SPEND ON EDUCATION NEXT YEAR. HE HOPES TO DO THAT TONIGHT.
MORE NEWS AFTER THIS MESSAGE:

(The copy in Item 4 is a "tag" or "button," a quick item that serves to round out a story.)

5.   FIRST   COMMERCIAL
(BLANK OIL COMPANY)
     VT - 10
     RUNS 1:00

6. DJ & RP
     (MAP, SOUTHEAST ASIA)

THE SOUTHEAST ASIAN NEWS BUDGET IS CROWDED TODAY...AS USUAL.

166

POP ON
(CROSS HATCH)

IN BANGKOK, THE FOREIGN MINISTERS OF SEATO, THE SOUTHEAST ASIAN TREATY ORGANIZATION, OPENED THEIR ANNUAL REVIEW OF MILITARY AND POLITICAL DEVELOPMENTS IN THE AREA.

U.S. SECRETARY OF STATE WARREN FRIEND IS SCHEDULED TO SPEAK TOMMOROW.

-0-

6A. DJ & RP
   (S.E.A. MAP CONT'D)

THERE WERE REPORTS OF DIFFERENT KINDS OF MILITARY MOVEMENTS TODAY IN LAOS AND THAILAND.

POP ON
(CIRCLE)

LAOTIAN GOVERNMENT FORCES WERE PULLED BACK FROM A VILLAGE FIFTY MILES NORTH OF LUANG PRABANG WHEN REPORTS OF COMMUNIST EFFORTS TO TAKE OVER THE VILLAGE DIDN'T CHECK OUT.

-0-

6B. DJ & RP
   (S.E.A. MAP CONT'D)

THE TROOP MOVEMENT IN THAILAND INVOLVED UNITED STATES' FORCES.

POP ON
(CROSS HATCH)

THE DEPARTMENT OF DEFENSE ANNOUNCED THAT FIVE-HUNDRED MORE AMERICAN SERVICEMEN WILL BE BROUGHT HOME FROM THE UDORN AIR BASE BY THE END OF THIS MONTH AS PART OF THE PROGRAM TO PHASE OUT U.S. MILITARY OPERATIONS THERE.

6C. DJ

THE AREA OF THE MOST RECENT MAJOR U.S. MILITARY INVOLVEMENT OFFERS SOME INTERESTING NEW CONTRASTS.

WE GET THAT STORY NOW FROM X.Y.Z. CORRESPONDENT ART SMITH:

7. SMITH FILM
   16-4—16-6
   RUNS 3:00
   (VIDEO)
(People building wooden houses. Flurry of activity. Establish for :10, then Smith walks into frame.)

IN CUE: IN THIS VILLAGE IN SOUTH VIET NAM RECONSTRUCTION IS THE NAME OF THE GAME...AND THE PEOPLE ARE HAPPY TO PLAY!

IT WAS A LONG WAR HERE.

THE OLDER VILLAGERS ...THOSE WHO'VE SEEN THIRTY BIRTHDAYS OR MORE...HARDLY CAN REMEMBER TIMES LIKE THESE...WHEN THE GUNS ARE SILENT AND ONE DOESN'T LIVE UNDER CONSTANT THREAT.

THE YOUNGER ONES NEVER KNEW WHAT PEACE WAS LIKE.

(Close ups of faces as people work at all sorts of tasks.)

THIS VILLAGE WAS ONE OF THE PAWNS OF WAR. GOVERNMENT FORCES HELD IT. THE VIET CONG TOOK IT OVER. GOVERNMENT TROOPS TOOK IT BACK.

NOBODY HEREABOUTS REMEMBERS JUST HOW MANY TIMES THE VILLAGE CHANGED HANDS...LIKE THE LEAD IN A CLOSE BASEBALL GAME.

NOW, HAPPILY, ALL THAT'S PAST...AND THERE'S EVEN TIME FOR A REAL BASEBALL GAME:

168

(People cheer as Viet Namese man hits ball and runs bases.)

(NATURAL SOUND OF GAME :10)

CHIN THU LEARNED TO HIT FROM THE U.S. MARINES. THAT WAS AFTER THE FIGHTING STOPPED...AND THE REBUILDING BEGAN.

WHEN THE GEE-EYES WEREN'T SHOWING THE VILLAGERS HOW TO HAMMER NAILS AND TO SAW TWO-BY-FOURS, THEY WERE TEACHING THEM SOMETHING ABOUT HITTING BASEBALLS AND FIELDING THEM.

THERE EVEN WAS TIME, THEN, FOR SOME AMERICAN SERVICEMEN TO LEARN TO SPEAK A LITTLE VIET NAMESE...AND VICE VERSA.

BECAUSE OF HIS ABILITY TO LEARN LOTS OF THINGS...HAMMERING NAILS AND SPEAKING ENGLISH INCLUDED...NGUYEN NGUYEN QUICKLY BECAME A KIND OF FOREMAN IN THIS VILLAGE'S RECONSTRUCTION PROGRAM:

(Two shot: Nguyen & Smith)

(SMITH) HOW'S IT GOING HERE?

(NGUYEN) FINE...FINE. ALREADY THREE HOUSES ARE UP. WE HAVE MANY PIECES OF WOOD...AND THE GOVERNMENT PROMISES TO SEND MORE.

(SMITH) IS THE GOVERN- MENT LIVING UP TO ITS PROMISES THESE DAYS?

169

(NGUYEN) PRETTY GOOD...PRETTY GOOD. SURE, WE'D LIKE TO GET MORE WOOD AND NAILS AND STUFF. BUT PEOPLE HERE ARE USED TO THE OLD DAYS...HARD TIMES YOUR GEE-EYES CALLED THEM. NOBODY'S UPSET. JUST WANT TO DO THE WORK...HAVE NICE, NEW, WOODEN HOUSES TO LIVE IN. GONNA BE GREAT HERE SOME DAY SOON.

(Pan street and houses.)

(SMITH) SOME DAY IS RIGHT. THERE ARE ONE-HUNDRED PEOPLE IN THIS VILLAGE AND THE MEN, WOMEN AND CHILDREN ALL PITCH IN TO DO WHATEVER THEY CAN.

(Close up: Boy digs with spoon.)

EVEN LITTLE NGUYEN HAS CAUGHT THE SPIRIT OF THE REBUILDING PROGRAM. AND, IN THIS CONTRY, THERE'LL BE WORK WAITING FOR HIM WHEN HE GROWS UP.

(Smith on camera with house in background)

MANY AN AMERICAN SERVICEMAN PASSED THROUGH HERE WHEN THE WAR WAS ON. THE ONLY VIVID RECOLLECTION ANYONE COULD HAVE CARRIED AWAY FROM HERE THEN WAS THAT OF A VILLAGE WHOSE NATURAL BEAUTY WAS A CAMOUFLAGE FOR CONSTANT DANGER.

TODAY, THAT'S ALL CHANGED. THE PEOPLE SMILE...AND MEAN IT. CAMOUFLAGE ISN'T NEEDED. AND HOUSES SOON WILL BE HOMES.

OUT CUE: ART SMITH, X.Y.Z. NEWS, IN A VILLAGE IN SOUTH VIET NAM.

8. DJ

THAT VILLAGE, OF COURSE, DOES NOT REPRESENT ALL OF SOUTH VIET NAM. AND THE QUESTION OF HOW EFFECTIVELY U.S. AID IS USED THERE IS RAISED ONCE AGAIN IN WASHINGTON.

X.Y.Z. CONGRESSIONAL CORRESPONDENT, ROY GREEN, SPOKE TO REPUBLICAN SENATOR JOE JONES OF IDAHO:

9. JONES INTERVIEW
   VT-8
   RUNS 2:40

IN CUE: (GREEN) SENATOR JONES, YOU'VE JUST...

(TRANSCRIPT)

returned from a visit to South Viet Nam...what impressions did you bring back about the aid programs there?

(JONES) Well, Mister Green, I can't honestly say I'm too happy. Oh, of course, there are areas of model achievements. That's where the public relations fellows rush you immediately. Those are the areas where things really look good, but the picture, overall, just isn't that good.

(GREEN) What specific faults did you find?

(JONES) The usual bureaucratic faults. You know, too much paperwork. Great, streamlined programs are put together...on paper, then go right into a file drawer and get buried under more and more tons of paper. An aid officer puts in his year of duty and is transferred to another post. You can't blame him for wanting to take the next step up his career ladder, but the programs he handled suffer.

(GREEN) Are those the main faults you found?

(JONES) The main ones, yes. But there are more. Frankly, I just can't escape the feeling that we're spending too much money there. We put our domestic economy in a bind for long years fighting the war. Now, that's over...but we're still spending half of what we spent to prosecute the war. Domestic programs still suffer.

(GREEN) Senator Jones, haven't we heard pretty much that same complaint from members of your party for years? After all, you've the reputation of a tight money man, aren't you just singing the dollar blues?

(JONES) No, Mister Green, I'm not just crying about money, but I admit I think we've spent enough on Viet Nam. It's an area that must be downgraded more and more each year in our budget. There are too many areas where our help is more urgently needed now. We must move on. We must put our own country to rights. You know all the old problems...air pollution, water pollution, mismanagement of natural resources. I could go on and on.

(GREEN) Well, then Senator Jones, what specifically do you recommend for South Viet Nam?

(JONES) I recommend phased financial withdrawal ...just the way we pulled the troops out. Sure, there are American soldiers still in South Viet Nam, but only a handful by comparison to three or four years ago. Let's do the same with U.S. dollars...pull 'em out gradually and let Saigon learn to stand on its own. I think it must be this way and the sooner the better.

(GREEN) Thank you. That was Republican Senator Joe Jones of Idaho, who's just returned from an inspection tour of South Viet Nam.

OUT CUE: THIS IS ROY GREEN, X.Y.Z. NEWS, WASHINGTON.

10. SECOND COMMERCIAL
(GULPO DOG FOOD)
    VT-10
    RUNS 1:00

11. DJ & RP (PLANE)	WOULD YOU BELIEVE THAT TWENTY-SIX PEOPLE WALKED AWAY FROM THAT?
	THAT'S THE WRECKAGE OF A SUPER AIRLINES JET THAT WAS INVOLVED IN A MID-AIR COLLISION TODAY WITH A SMALL, PRIVATE PLANE.
	HAPPILY, EVERYONE SURVIVED.
12. PLANE CRASH FILM RUNNING IN RP SCREEN DJ-VO :30	THE JETLINER HAD JUST TAKEN OFF FROM IN-TERNATIONAL AIR-PORT...FOR MIAMI.
	THE PILOT, CAPTAIN RON BETZ, SAID THERE WAS A MOMENTARY BREAK IN HIS RADIO CONTACT WITH THE CONTROL TOWER. WHEN THE RECEPTION CLEARED, BETZ SAID, HE HEARD THE TOWER WARNING HIM THAT A SMALL PLANE WAS CLOSING FROM BEHIND.
	BETZ TOOK IMMEDIATE EVASIVE ACTION, BUT LOST MUCH OF HIS RIGHT WING. STILL, HE WAS ABLE TO LAND THE JET WITHOUT SERIOUS INJURY TO ANYONE ABOARD.
	JUST AFTER THE PLANE WAS EVACUATED, FIRE BROKE OUT AND DEMOLISH-ED IT.

(It would be unusual for a cameraman to be on hand to film such a drama as it is happening. In this case, then, the silent film to be voiced-over would be aftermath material such as the burning wreckage and perhaps firemen at work. Still, the film is useful for background over which the newscaster can tell the story of what happened.)

13. DJ

THAT PLANE CRASH REPORT IS UNUSUAL...IN THE SENSE OF SURVIVAL OF ALL THE PASSENGERS AND CREW.

WITH THE INCREASING INCIDENCE OF MID-AIR COLLISIONS, X.Y.Z. NEWS SENT REPORTER CHUCK O'BRIEN TO LEARN WHAT NEW STEPS ARE BEING TAKEN TO AVOID THE DANGER:

14. F.A.A. FILM (O'BRIEN)
    16-6—16-8
    RUNS 3:10

(Film opens with
   O'Brien on camera in
   front of a building.)

IN CUE: WHEN YOU WANT TO FIND OUT WHAT'S GOING ON IN THE FIELD OF AIR TRAVEL, THIS IS THE PLACE TO COME.

THIS IS HEADQUARTERS FOR THE FEDERAL AD-MINISTRATION.

THE MAN IN CHARGE OF COORDINATING ALL THE EFFORTS OF BOTH THE GOVERNMENT AND THE COMMERCIAL AIRLINES IN CUTTING DOWN THE RISK OF MID-AIR COLLISIONS IS

(Dissolve to Collins)

AVERY COLLINS. I ASKED HIM ABOUT REPORTS OF A NEW RADAR DEVICE TO WARN PILOTS:

(COLLINS) WE'RE EN-COURAGED, MISTER

(TRANSCRIPT)

O'BRIEN. It's been a long, difficult, and until now, troubled search. But, we had the benefit recently of a real breakthrough in miniaturization of the electronic gear a safety system requires and now we think we're really on our way.

(O'BRIEN) Could you give us more detail, Mister Collins?

(COLLINS) Surely. As you know, we've been hung up for years trying to develop an air safety system that is both sensitive enough to provide real protection for both commercial airliners and private planes and that, at the same time, is in a cost area that makes it practical. Originally, you know, that is to say four or five years ago, we had a workable device. It was workable from the standpoint that if two planes on a collision course were equipped with the detection device there would never have been any real danger. They'd have had more than enough time to take evasive action without any trouble. The problem, of course, was that the device was really too large for most private planes and much, much too costly to expect widespread use. It was running then at a cost of about fifty-thousand dollars for the device, plus a heavy installation cost. Totally prohibitive, you know.

(O'BRIEN) And now you think those problems have been solved?

(COLLINS) We're farther along the road than that, Mister O'Brien. Matter of fact, I can give you a graphic demonstration of just how far along we really are.

(At this point, an ordinary, face-to-camera interview can effectively be turned into a true television news story, a pictorial story, by the use of silent film on a sound projector. Often, an interview subject such as our mythical Mister Collins will be discussing something that can be filmed. When the subject reaches a suitable point in the interview, the silent film can be played against the subject's own description as in this example:)

(COLLINS CONTINUED) Right here in the F.A.A. building, we have a working model of our new system, with a mock up of a 747 jetliner and a small private plane. In our model, the jetliner is climbing away from an airport. Five miles away, at five-thousand feet and on the exact course, is our small plane. Neither pilot has the visibility to see the other plane, but there's no cause for alarm now. The gray boxes in both cabins take care of this problem. When the planes are three miles apart on an unmistakable collision course, a buzzer sounds. (Here there would be natural sound of the buzzer.) It is loud enough and annoying enough to make sure no pilot ever could miss the warning. And, there's ample time to avert a tragedy.

(O'BRIEN) That's an effective demonstration, Mister Collins. But how soon will these devices be ready to use?

(COLLINS) They're on the assembly line right now. It's taken us a long time to get what we wanted and many lives have been lost while these devices were being perfected. But we now have the legislation to make the airlines and private plane owners equip their aircraft with these remarkable instruments. I can tell you this in all confidence and sincerity. Mister O'Brien. The day of the mid-air collision

OUT CUE: ...WILL BE OVER WITHIN ANOTHER YEAR.

(That prediction would be a dramatic point to get out of the film. Reporter O'Brien had, of course, done a complete job, with his on camera close and sign-off, but this is a case in which the production staff wants the dramatic impact of the interview subject's own words to wind things up and this is accomplished smoothly by having the anchor man "tag" or "button" the film in some manner such as this;)

15. DJ	A PLEDGE OF NEW SAFETY FOR AIR TRAVELERS FROM THE MAN WHO SHOULD KNOW...AVERY COLLINS, AIR SAFETY COORDINATOR FOR THE FEDERAL AVIATION ADMINISTRATION.

-0-

15A. DJ & RP (ASTRONAUTS)	ASTRONAUTS PAUL MILLER AND BILL PERCY HAD SAFETY IN MIND...THEIR OWN, THAT IS...WHEN THEY WENT THROUGH FINAL TEST DOCKING MANEUVERS THIS AFTERNOON. MILLER AND PERCY ARE SCHEDULED TO LIFT OFF NEXT WEDNESDAY MORNING ON A TEN-DAY EARTH OR-BITAL FLIGHT IN WHICH THEY'LL LINK THEIR SPACE

CRAFT WITH ANOTHER SENT UP ONE DAY BEFORE. AFTER THE SHIPS ARE JOINED, MILLER AND PERCY WILL WELD THEM TOGETHER TO MAKE THE FIRST STAGE OF A NEW ORBITING SPACE LABORATORY.

TODAY'S SIMULATION AT NATIONAL AERONAUTICS AND SPACE AGENCY HEADQUARTERS IN HOUSTON WAS PRONOUNCED A COMPLETE SUCCESS, NASA SPOKESMEN SAID. IN FACT, THE ASTRONAUTS ARE READY TO GO RIGHT NOW, BUT THAT THE FINAL PROGRAMMED TESTS WILL BE CARRIED OUT ALL THE WAY...SIMPLY FOR SAFETY.

-0-

15B. DJ

WEST GERMANY SAYS...NO.

THE SOVIET UNION SAYS...YES.

AND, THE BRITISH SAY MAYBE!

A CLOSER LOOK AT THOSE STORIES AFTER THIS MESSAGE:

16. THIRD COMMERCIAL (X.Y.Z. NETWORK COMEDY HOUR)
VT - 10
RUNS 1:00

17. DJ & RP
(SCHOLTZ)

WEST GERMAN CHANCELLOR EUGENE SCHOLTZ TODAY REJECTED A NEW FRENCH PROPOSAL TO

177

DISBAND THE PRESENT EUROPEAN COMMON MARKET IN FAVOR OF A TWO-NATION ECONOMIC ALLIANCE.

SCHOLTZ SAID HE HAD THE COMPLETE SUPPORT OF ALL POLITICAL ELEMENTS WITHIN HIS COUNTRY IN REFUSING THE FRENCH BID. HE SAID SUCH A MOVE COULD ONLY PROVE DIVISIVE FOR THE CONTINENT OF EUROPE.

-0-

17A DJ & RP
(MAP: RUSSIA-
CHINA BORDER)

POP ON
(BORDER LINE)

POP ON
(ROCKET)

THE SOVIET UNION TODAY ANNOUNCED THAT IT WILL ACCEPT A UNITED NATIONS' REQUEST TO WITH-DRAW ITS TROOPS FROM THE LONG-DISPUTED AREA ALONG THE BORDER OF COMMUNIST CHINA'S SINKIANG PROVINCE.

THE TERRITORY HAS BEEN THE SCENE OF FREQUENT FIGHTING BET-WEEN THE TWO NATIONS.

IT'S AN AREA OF PAR-TICULAR SENSITIVITY TO THE PEKING GOVERNMENT BECAUSE OF THE CHINESE NUCLEAR FACILITY AT LOP NOR, ONLY SOME THREE-HUNDRED MILES FROM THE BORDER.

-0-

17B. DJ & RP
(PARLIAMENT)

THE BRITISH HOUSE OF COMMONS TODAY GAVE TENTATIVE APPROVAL TO THE GOVERNMENT'S PLAN TO SPEND FIVE-BILLION

178

DOLLARS IN THE NEXT TWO YEARS TO MODERNIZE THE COUNTRY'S HIGHWAY SYSTEM.

THE NEW SUM WOULD REPRESENT BRITAIN'S SECOND MAJOR EXPENDITURE ON HIGHWAYS WITHIN THREE YEARS.

X.Y.Z.'S CORRESPONDENT IN LONDON, ARNOLD PIERCE, REPORTS ON PROGRESS TO DATE IN THE BRITISH CAPITAL:

18. BRITISH TRAFFIC
    (PIERCE)
    VT-8
    RUNS 2:15

(TAPE BEGINS WITH SCENE OF TV SCREEN AND TWO MEN SEATED AT CONTROL PANELS, WITH NATURAL SOUND.)

IN CUE: THIS IS WHAT LONDON TRAFFIC LOOKS LIKE IN THE FIVE O'CLOCK RUSH HOUR...ON A TELEVISION SCREEN, ANYWAY!

IT'S A GRIM PICTURE...BUT BETTER TO LOOK AT IT ON TV THAN TO BE OUT IN IT!

(CLOSE UP SCREEN AND FLASHING LIGHTS)

ACTUALLY, THIS CLOSED-CIRCUIT TV SURVEILLANCE SYSTEM IS THE FIRST MODERN THING THAT'S HAPPENED TO TRAFFIC IN THE WORLD'S THIRD LARGEST CITY IN THIRTY YEARS. THAT WAS WHEN THE LAST NEW ROADS WERE BUILT HERE.

THE SYSTEM IS THE WORLD'S FIRST ATTEMPT TO CONTROL TRAFFIC FLOW BY COMPUTER. THE SYSTEM WAS DEVISED THREE YEARS

AGO WHEN DESPERATE BRITONS FINALLY DECIDED TO TRY TO GET HIGHWAY TRAFFIC ROLLING AGAIN.

THE MAN WHO RUNS THIS SYSTEM IS NICK COEN: ...We think it's going well.

(TRANSCRIPT)

This system controls traffic signals on about six miles of streets through west London. The system has been in use only one year, but already we've cut travel time at peak traffic hours by nine percent.''

(TRAFFIC SCENES)

COEN IS HOPEFUL, BUT HE KNOWS HOW MUCH REMAINS TO BE DONE...AND THAT'S PLENTY.

THERE ARE EIGHT MILLION PEOPLE IN LONDON. THE LAST TRAFFIC SURVEY MADE HERE TEN YEARS AGO FORECAST THAT PRIVATE OWNERSHIP OF AUTOS WOULD MORE THAN DOUBLE IN TEN YEARS...TO TWO-AND-A-HALF MILLION VEHICLES. BUT NOTHING WAS DONE.

(NARROW STREETS)

BASIC TO LONDON'S TRAFFIC PROBLEM ARE THE STREETS. MANY PERMIT THE PASSAGE OF ONLY ONE CAR AT A TIME...THROUGH A TANGLE OF SEVENTEENTH AND EIGHTEENTH CENTURY ROADS THAT PROBABLY WERE INADEQUATE EVEN TO THE HORSE AND BUGGY.

(SHOPPING AREA)

THESE VILLAGES WITHIN LONDON ARE A PROBLEM IN THEMSELVES AS FAR AS TRAFFIC GOES, BUT THE SHOPPING DISTRICTS ARE EVEN WORSE. OXFORD STREET, FOR EXAMPLE, IS LONDON'S MAIN SHOPPING ARTERY. A LEADING BRITISH

TRAFFIC CONSULTANT ONCE DESCRIBED IT AS "THE MOST UNCIVILIZED STREET IN EUROPE." HE WAS REFERRING NOT TO THE STORES, BUT RATHER TO THE CLASH OF PEDESTRIAN AND AUTO TRAFFIC.

(PIERCE ON CAMERA)

LONDON IS FULL OF HISTORY. TOO FULL, IN FACT, TO ACCOMMODATE SUCH TWENTIETH CENTURY PHENOMENA AS THE AUTO EXPLOSION.

BUT, A COMPUTER COMPLEX ON THE WEST SIDE OF LONDON AND MASSIVE NEW INJECTIONS OF MONEY TO GET A START ON A MODERN ROAD SYSTEM IN-DICATE THAT THE STURDY AND RESOLUTE BRITISH ARE BEGINNING TO FIGHT OFF THE LATEST SIEGE OF LONDON.

OUT CUE: ARNOLD PIERCE, X.Y.Z. NEWS, LONDON.

-0-

19. DJ

HERE AT HOME, WORLDWIDE COMPUTERS INCORPORATED AND DATA UNLIMITED TODAY REVEALED PLANS TO MERGE IN A MOVE THAT WOULD CREATE A NEW GIANT IN THE FIELD OF ELECTRONIC DATA

-0-

19A. DJ & RP
(MARKET)

ON WALL STREET TODAY, PRICES WERE SUB-STANTIALLY HIGHER IN HEAVY TRADING.

THE DOW-JONES IN-DUSTRIAL AVERAGE CLOSED AT NINE-HUNDRED-AND-EIGHTY-SEVEN POINT NINETY-SEVEN...UP TEN POINT TWENTY-THREE.

-0-

19B. DJ

SOMETHING NEW AND DIFFERENT WAS ADDED TODAY TO THE MAYORAL CONTEST IN LOS ANGELES. BILL ARTHUR HAS THE STORY:

20. CALIFORNIA POLITICS
(ARTHUR)
   16-2—16-4
   RUNS 1:45

IN CUE: CITY HALL HERE HAS BEEN OCCUPIED BY SOME EXTRAORDINARY FIGURES IN RECENT TIMES. BUT YOU CAN TEAR UP THE BOOK IF THE LATEST ENTRY IN A FIFTEEN—CANDIDATE RACE MAKES THE GRADE.

(ELLINGTON AT CITY CLERK'S OFFICE)

BARTON ELLINGTON TODAY PRODUCED A PETITION WITH ENOUGH NAMES TO QUALIFY HIM TO RUN AND THE NECESSARY FEE TO REGISTER AS A CANDIDATE.

ELLINGTON DIDN'T TAKE TIME TO CAMPAIGN RIGHT OFF...BECAUSE HE HAD TO

(ELLINGTON AT WORK)

GET BACK TO THE LOS ANGELES ZOO. HIS POLITICAL ACTIVITY FOR TODAY WAS CONFINED TO HIS LUNCH HOUR.

THE THIRTY-SEVEN YEAR-OLD ELLINGTON IS IN CHARGE OF THE MONKEY HOUSE AT THE ZOO...AND THE MONKEYS WON'T DELAY THEIR DINNER FOR POLITICS.

182

AFTER HIS CHARGES HAD BEEN FED. I ASKED ELLINGTON WHY HE THOUGHT HE COULD RUN A CITY...ANY CITY...ESPECIALLY ONE THE SIZE OF LOS ANGLELES?

(ELLINGTON) Some people think I've been...

(TRANSCRIPT)

around the apes too long. They think my venture into politics is nothing but monkey business, if you'll pardon the expression. I don't consider it that at all and I've managed in two short weeks to get twenty-five hundred people to book me up. You saw the petition I filed this afternoon. I'm in this race to stay!

(ARTHUR) You didn't answer my question, Mister Ellington. What do you think qualifies you to run for Mayor?

(ELLINGTON) Sorry about that. I got carried away. Mister Arthur, I'm thoroughly convinced that the regular sociological patterns in a city this size are overwhelming and completely misunderstood. There are so many people in Los Angeles that things just aren't getting done. It's mostly a problem of discipline. Now, here at the Zoo, we have a similar situation. I've had plenty of opportunity to study how the monkeys handle their problems. When they can't seem to work things out for themselves. I've learned to divert them from hostile behavior to tolerant, patient attempts to solve problems. If I can do that with the monkeys, I think I can help people, too.

(Arthur on Camera)

WELL, THEY'VE TRIED LOTS OF THINGS IN CALIFORNIA POLITICS...BUT A MASTER OF MONKEY PSYCHOLOGY SURELY QUALIFIES AS SOMETHING OF

A DEPARTURE...EVEN IN CALIFORNIA.

OUT CUE: BILL ARTHUR, X.Y.Z. NEWS, LOS ANGELES

-0-

21. DJ

THAT ELECTION IN LOS ANGELES IS SCHEDULED FOR TWO WEEKS FROM NEXT TUESDAY. AND, WITH FIF-TEEN CANDIDATES IN THE FIELD, A RUN-OFF SEEMS CERTAIN.

X.Y.Z. NEWS WILL KEEP YOU INFORMED...ABOUT MISTER ELLINGTON AND THE OTHERS INVOLVED.

-0-

I'LL HAVE MORE NEWS IN A MOMENT:

(Item 21 represents another kind of tag for a pictorial report. Earlier, in Item 15, a few words were needed because there was no sign-off to the report. In this case, the tag is used for the purpose of informing the viewers. Nowhere in Arthur's report was there any mention of the time element involved in the election. It is natural then for the anchor man to come back and provide missing bits of useful information, which may have been left out or cut out.)

22. FOURTH COMMERCIAL
(BLANK COFFEE)
    VT - 10
    RUNS 1:00

23. DJ

TWO GIRLS, TWO BOYS AND TWO GUITARS ADDED UP TO A LOT OF NOISE...AND CONFUSION...TODAY IN PITTSBURGH.

JIM BROWN HAS THAT STORY:

24.   PITTSBURGH   FILM
(BROWN)
  16-4—16-6
  RUNS 2:00

....**IN CUE: A HARD ROCK GROUP CALLING ITSELF** "THE CLUMSY OAFS HIT TOWN TODAY...AND THE IMPACT WAS HEARD FOR MILES AROUND.

(NATURAL SOUND OF MUSIC :10)

(PAN GROUP FACES)

THE WANDERING MINSTRELS WANDERED RIGHT UP TO THE STAGE DOOR OF THE PITTSBURGHER THEATER AND CASUALLY WALKED RIGHT IN. THEY

(PEOPLE WAITING)

SAID THEY SAW THE LINE OF PATRONS OUTSIDE THE THEATER WAITING TO BUY TICKETS AND JUST THOUGHT TO THEMSELVES, HOW VERY NICE!

(CLOSE UP: PICK)

ONE OF THE GUITARISTS IDENTIFIED HIMSELF AS RICK PICK AND INSISTED HE WAS THE BIGGEST OAF...OR DID HE SAY THE HEAD OAF? AT ANY RATE, PICK SAID HE PICKED UP HIS FIRST REAL HINT THAT SOMETHING WAS AMISS WHEN HE AND HIS

(THRU DOOR & INSIDE)

"CLUMSY OAF" ASSOCIATES WALKED INTO THE EMPTY DRESSING ROOMS WITH THE STARS ON THE DOOR. HE ADMITTED THE CROWD OUTSIDE AND THE STAR TREATMENT WERE THINGS THEY JUST WEREN'T EXPECTING. BUT, SAID PICK, THIS WAS THEIR FIRST BIG DATE IN A BIG TOWN AND HE JUST FIGURED THIS WAS THE WAY IT IS DONE.

(THRU WINGS)

IN KEEPING WITH THEIR OWN QUITE CASUAL STYLE,

(VIEW FROM STAGE)

"THE CLUMSY OAFS" SIMPLY FELL INTO FORMATION IN THE THEATER WINGS...BEGAN STRUMMING THEIR INSTRUMENTS AND SINGING...AND SAUNTERED ONTO THE STAGE.

AS PICK LATER EXPLAINED, HE WAS ABSOLUTELY CERTAIN THAT SOMETHING REALLY WAS WRONG WHEN "THE CLUMSY OAFS" PEERED FROM THE STAGE INTO A THEATER WITH NO ONE IN IT.

IN THE MEANTIME, THE RACKET THEY CREATED ON STAGE BROUGHT THE MANAGER, WHO STOOD IN STUNNED AMAZEMENT ON SEEING THE SOLITARY, SHAGGY GROUP.

THE ON-STAGE MEETING OF "THE CLUMSY OAFS" AND THE THEATER MANAGER FINALLY GOT THE PROBLEM WORKED OUT.

IT WAS TRUE, ALL RIGHT. "THE CLUMSY OAFS" WERE EXPECTED TO TAKE PART IN A HARD ROCK RALLY...IN THE PITTSBURGHER THEATER... ONE MONTH FROM TODAY.

(NATURAL SOUND MUSIC :10)

(BROWN ON CAMERA WITH GROUP MARCHING AWAY AND PLAYING)

THUS, THE PEOPLE IN DOWNTOWN PITTSBURGH WERE TREATED TO A SMALL, IMPROMPTU BUT NOISY PARADE AS THE ROCK GROUP MARCHED BACK FROM THE THEATER TO THE BUS DEPOT...TO GO BACK HOME

AND REHEARSE A LITTLE WHILE LONGER.

WHAT FEW PEDESTRIANS KNEW AT THE TIME WAS THAT THEY WERE LISTENING TO AND LOOKING AT "THE CLUMSY OAFS."

JIM BROWN, X.Y.Z. NEWS, PITTSBURGH.

-0-

25. DJ

AND, ONCE AGAIN, THE OLD QUESTION "WHAT'S IN A NAME" IS ANSWERED!

-0-

THAT'S THE EVENING NEWS FOR THIS WEDNESDAY, OCTOBER TENTH.

THIS IS DAVE JOHNSON. GOOD EVENING FROM THE ENTIRE X.Y.Z. NEWS STAFF

26. FIFTH COMMERCIAL (BLANK SOFT DRINK)
    VT - 10
    RUNS 1:00

-0-

27. CLOSE AND ANNOUNCE

16-4
(AGAIN, THE CLOSING SOUND FILM WOULD BE THE STANDARD EVEN-ING NEWS MUSICAL SIGNATURE, WITH A STAFF ANNOUNCER VOICE OVER)

THE X.Y.Z. EVENING NEWS, A ROUND-UP OF EVENTS ACROSS THE NATION AND AROUND THE WORLD, IS BROUGHT TO YOU MONDAY THROUGH FRIDAY.

THE ENTIRE PRODUC-TION IS SUPERVISED AND CONTROLLED BY X.Y.Z. NEWS, INCORPORATED.

It should be emphasized again that there is no single, right way to treat a newscast, or even a news story. Given the preceding artificial newscast's various elements, ten producers surely would have handled them in at least eight and probably ten different ways. Similarly, ten correspondents ordinarily will come up with ten varying treatments of the same news story. This is not to imply any loose handling of the facts but rather to indicate the subjective considerations of television and, for that matter, any other kind of news coverage. It is true, of course, that certain news stories have an obvious logic and thus fall into a pattern. The same can be said of the newscast; certain items and elements go naturally together and to separate them is to destroy a logical flow.

One of the great charms and certainly one of the keenest challenges of television news is the broad latitude it leaves at both the editorial and production stages. Effort and imagination open all sorts of avenues for interesting and unusual presentation of news on television.

CHAPTER 14

Anchoring the TV Newscast

There's a basic sort of contradication about television news: It is the most intimate form yet devised for informing great masses of people! On the television screen, the reporter's byline leaps from print into life; he is an eyewitness to history, bringing his account of that happening into the home during or shortly after the event occurs. Often, a happening that captures the interest of millions unfolds before the viewer's eyes, with a trained journalist in attendance to tell almost everything that is known or can be envisioned about that event and to help put it into perspective. The owner of the television set can sit comfortably at home and draw the information he needs to form his own opinions about his world from another individual in a basically isolated but a seemingly person-to-person relationship.

To the basic contradiction of the medium itself is added the further contradication in the methods by which television news is gathered and disseminated at its lowest and highest levels. The newsman at the local independent station must make the most of often drastically limited resources; his network counterpart is a virtual prince with a wealth of human help, material and facilities available to help him do his work well. The management of many local stations sometimes appears to be trying to make it difficult to get news on the air, while the corporate leadership of the networks is not allowed to forget for long its responsibility in the areas of news and public affairs.

Mention already has been made of how very much one man can be called upon to do at the local television station. It is obvious that, in some instances, news is nothing more than a necessary evil that eats into the corporate profits. Therefore, the management will hire as few persons as it can just to do enough to protect its franchise. On the other hand, many local educational stations undertake the task of covering broad areas where no commercial television service exists and fall far short of adequate performance for the valid reason that they do not have a sufficient budget to hire the people they would like to employ to do the job well.

Frequently, the total responsibility for the small station's news output is vested in the person of the news director, who is expected to plan the local coverage, make certain it is carried out and, finally, to bring the finished product before the camera. It also has been noted often enough that this superhuman might be called upon to participate in various ways in the shooting and editing of film. The stark reality that this is too much for any one human is recognized by most station managements, but some remain content to let it go at that. In these generally unnecessary, poverty-line TV news operations, manpower limitations almost always are accompanied by extremely restricted facilities. That's part of the same, sorry game.

The news director must get to the station in time to check out what is happening that day and lay out the stories he wants covered. If he has a cameraman, he must take time to explain to him what he wants covered and in what way. Budgetary restrictions can be so tight that the news director actually must allot a certain amount of film footage to each story, or it could be that he knows his own air requirements so well as to be able to estimate closely how much film time he will be able to devote to a particular item. The marvel of this kind of broadcast journalism is that so much is produced with so little. It is the resourcefulness of the individual that carries the situation.

While the day's newsfilm is being shot and processed, the news director in the one-man operation must pursue the often arduous routine of gathering news and keeping up with what is happening in his area. Unless there is an occurrence of at least state-wide importance, he will get little in the way of assistance from the wire services, which aren't geared to servicing the needs of individual stations. The local news director must be able to get out and around town, perhaps even to cover a daily "beat," to keep his lines of communication open to local officials: they are the sources of news.

When he is in the newsroom, he must check wire service reports regularly to make certain he knows what is going on and to double check that an important story hasn't broken under his nose without his knowing about it. Then, with some idea of how the day is shaping up, he can begin to lay out the day's newscast and to write it, assuming there is one major production to which he is pointing. It is entirely conceivable, of course, that his responsibility may reach to two or more shorter newscasts, but most stations that do produce news coverage of their area tend to put on at least one longer newscast each weekday, a production running at least 15 minutes. More active stations often follow the pattern of producing half-hour local newscasts to dovetail with the evening network newscasts and thus provide a full hour of news programming weekday evenings. Independent stations that are diligent about their news coverage also need more than quickie, five-minute newscasts to justify the expenditures they make for film coverage. Whatever the situation, the news director in the one-man news operation has put in a full day's work by the time he must be ready to broadcast.

Still another responsibility for every broadcaster, from the news-director-anchorman in the small town to the network newscaster, is that of checking all those difficult pronunciations he will run into. He shouldn't use words he can't pronounce in the first place, but when it comes to the names of individuals and places within his coverage area, difficult pronunciations are impossible to avoid. When a newsman covering a particular area can't take the time to learn the accepted way to say the name of a person or place, he is not doing his job properly. Personalities in the news, locally or otherwise, may be insulted by the mispronunciation of their names. Often someone at the station who grew up in the area can substitute for a pronouncing gazeteer. A telephone call to the personality or someone who knows him can produce the preferred pronunciation of the name. These are efforts that not only are worthwhile, but are absolutely essential. Mispronunciation of a name or a place will happen occasionally, but when the newsman says the same thing wrong regularly, it strikes at his credibility.

ANCHORING THE LOCAL NEWSCAST

The small-station news director who doubles as the anchorman just might, if he cares enough and has the time, put a bit of pancake makeup on his face before he goes into the studio to face the hot lights. In all probability, however, he will be more concerned with the need to sit down with his director to go over what he wants to do and how and when he wants to do it in order that there can be some degree of coordination on the air. The director, in turn, probably will be another do-it-himself sort who runs his own control board while giving whatever cues he has to whatever assistance he has, which, more than likely, consists of an audio man.

Once the tally light on the studio camera goes on, signaling the "performer" that he's on the air, it's a play-it-by-ear existence. If the news director is fortunate, he might have a monitor, or television receiver, built into the set or placed in some spot where he can make an occasional check of how things are progressing. Since much of what he does involves voice over film, he is at a dreadful disadvantage if he cannot see the film he is reading against. When he cannot see it, he must just hope he has timed it properly beforehand and that the film came up where he wanted it. He has no recourse.

As far as the timing of the production is concerned, there may be a clock on the studio wall nearby or he may have started his stopwatch when the tally light went on. In either case, it is difficult to concentrate on the copy and everything else at the same time. It is necessary to devise some system of time cues that the cameraman can work into his own busy routine. This often can be accomplished by making up cards with numerals indicating how many seconds remain to a commercial, for instance, or to the end of the production. Ordinarily, the cameraman is the key to handling timing problem on the air in that he has to be tied by internal communications to the control room and director or else he cannot possibly know what to do or when to do it. The cameraman ordinarily wears headphones through which he receives cues from the director. It is up to the anchorman and the cameraman to work out a set of signals that can be understood readily.

If something goes wrong on the air, the anchorman simply is stuck. He must be prepared, mentally, for minor disasters, such as a film break or an air reel of film put together out of proper sequence so that when he expects to read against one piece of film, something else comes up on the air. This sort of thing can throw anyone, but the newsman on television must be able to vamp his way out of difficulty. There just is no one there to help. He's out in front, by himself, and must fall back on his own personality and knowledge to get him through. It is an awkward situation at best. Perhaps a few words of explanation and apology are enough. Then the newsman should just forget about his immediate problem and get on with the production. It might be possible to go quickly to a commercial, which would allow one minute, usually, for the forces in trouble to regroup, but one minute isn't long and the performer and the director simply can't, stop at that moment, and formulate entirely new plans.

Again, the loss of either silent or sound film or video tape on the air has to create a timing problem. It is wise always to carry an extra minute's worth of copy into the studio to fend against just such a disaster, or else to have adequate "standby" copy containing at least a brief summary of what was on the sound element that was lost. In the case of silent film, the anchorman obviously has the copy to cover that film in his hand. It is because of the possibility of just this sort of problem that in writing television news copy, either for silent film or for still pictures, it is poor practice to refer directly to the pictorial element just in case it really is not there when it is supposed to be. Phrases such as "this film" or "as you see here" are built-in traps and the medium has enough traps of its own without adding any.

Obviously, the grim picture painted here is representative only of the thin side of the television news spectrum. As the people involved grow more responsible in their use of the medium and as competition increases, rag, tag and bobtail operations that function with only minimally standards will disappear. The irony in this kind of penny ante situation is that, more often than not, it winds up costing the management the money it is trying to save. First of all, the only arena in which a station can expect to get by on as little news as possible is in a purely non-competitive situation, where the viewer has no choice. With the passage of time, hopefully, these situations of monopoly operations will disappear. In the second place, it is costly to have to hire and train new people all the time and this often is the result of pinched operations. Newsmen with any kind of professional standards and pride soon grow frustrated in these situations and look elsewhere, and the turn-over cycle starts all over again. It is discouraging for the young newsman who sets out to do a good job to find himself trapped, at least momentarily. If he cannot bring management around to a more responsible point of view, he is better off removing himself to another, better station.

MEDIUM-SIZED STATION NEWSCAST

In between the "sweatshop" television news operations and the networks is a vast middle ground occupied by many stations who do their utmost to produce a worthy product and cover their local area properly. Often the responsible approach is dictated by a competitive situation, but there also are those genuinely interested operations that take enormous and justifiable pride in their news coverage. Here, too, it is a question, first of all, of hiring good people, paying them the sort of wages that not only will keep them happy but also anxious to grow in professional capability and keep up with modern trends in broadcast journalism, and the equipment needed to do the job right. Undeniably, this is expensive, but it is part of the pledge the owners of television stations make when they bid for a license.

One of the tremendous advantages the young newsman encounters as he climbs the professional ladder from the small to the medium-sized and more active station is the likelihood that he now will come under the guidance of an experienced news director and will come into contact, also, with other professionals who are on the same team and are trying to do a good job. Here, there will be time and the opportunity to compare techniques, to take advantage of constructive criticism, and perhaps to experiment with new ways to do things. If the newsman enters a competitive situation, he will come to analyze and know what the opposition is doing and will come under constant pressure to do his own work better. Whether he starts as a field reporter or plunges in right away as an anchorman, he will find himself constantly being compared to his opposite numbers. Few occupations provide the opportunities, or dangers, for such direct comparison that television news does. First of all, the reporter goes out to cover the story. If he is not diligent about the facts and his competitor is, he soon will be revealed for what he is. Then, too, there always are opportunities to bring more industry, energy, and imagination to news coverage. If the newsman's competitor constantly is more enterprising in the way he handles a story, the opposition always will look better and his own superiors will begin to wonder.

While newsmen in middle-sized stations are called upon to perform a variety of tasks, mostly they are related directly to the editorial side of news coverage. At this level, for instance, the newsman is not so likely to be caught up in photography. It is more likely here that when he is assigned to a story he will have a cameraman assigned with him who probably will handle the filming, process the film and then edit it in consultation with the reporter. It is a great advantage, of course, for the newsman to be able to concentrate on the editorial side of his story. He must be aware, however, of the cameraman's needs and must frame his film reportage with the cameraman's needs in mind. A wholesome working relationship between the reporter and the cameraman can make life and work much easier for both individuals and the end product much better for the station that employs them. The author was told recently of a cameraman, assigned to film a plane crash scene, who was so determined to carry out his task that he walked six miles through woods and mountains. He was rewarded for his diligence by making exclusive film of the disaster because no planes were available for aerial filming and no other cameramen were willing to make the trek. Imagine what a help someone of that ilk could be to a young reporter!

As the young newsman gathers experience in his new situation and learns how his new station wants things done, he probably will begin to draw the assignment of anchoring or perhaps co-anchoring various newscasts. Usually, the new man on the newscast has the lowest rating, which might mean he draws a weekend or early morning assignment. The time is not as important as the opportunity to gain experience and confidence in front of the camera. The practice of using two men to anchor the longer newscasts, those that run 15 minutes or half an hour, is common and does break up both the work load and the monotony of one face and one voice.

Here, again, the newcomer will be expected to gather the local news he is to report and write it for himself. His colleagues usually will provide him with the information he needs to write into or out of a piece of film or video tape, or else he must make arrangements to see the pictorial element, which is the wiser course anyhow. If he works for a network affiliate, he might be expected to monitor or look at the network newscast preceding his own local newscast and select portions that could be reused. In this case, he will run a stopwatch on at least the segments he knows he will want or perhaps the entire network production, taking in cues and out cues for an engineer to use later to edit the pieces out of the original, to make "dubs" or copies, or else to cue up the tape of the network feed so that it can be run into the local newscast with no editing at all.

If the newsman works for a network affiliate, he will have to be precise about timing his own newscast, especially if it precedes some kind of network production that would result in his being "clipped" off the air if he runs over his allotted time. At independent stations, time requirements are more flexible, but it still is sensible practice to time a newscast exactly and try to make it come out as planned. It is more than likely at the medium-sized station, also, that he will get additional help in timing and cueing from a floor manager. In this case, instead of relying on a busy cameraman for cues, the floor manager is there to coordinate activities in the control room with proceedings in the studio.

Here, again, the physical handling of the script is an important factor in the anchorman's effectiveness. Because he has written his own material, he starts out with a basic familiarity with the words before him. He must develop the habit of biting off sizable chunks of copy in his mind so that he can make sustained eye contact with the camera, thus creating the impression that he is talking, not reading. Occasional glances at the script are not only necessary but desirable because such head motion is normal in public speaking. By and large, script handling is a matter of personal preference, of practice and refining the technique that is most comfortable for the individual in front of the camera.

Occasionally, newsmen are called upon to broadcast a station editorial or some particularly sensitive piece of copy with which management doesn't wish to leave anything to chance. The station's artist or art department might then be asked to put all the copy for that item in large print on cue cards that can be held alongside the camera for the anchorman to read.

It might be, too, that as the newsman moves into the larger station he will encounter union contracts that define the limits of his responsibility and also stipulate minimum wage scales. For newsmen who do air work, the union that represents them is the American Federation of Television and Radio Artists (AFTRA), an AFL-CIO affiliated union that, as its name explains, represents a broad sweep of the men and women who are seen and heard on radio and television.

ANCHORING THE NETWORK NEWSCAST

In previous comparisons between the local and network news operations, mention has been made of the vast differences in resources, manpower, time and facilities available to the anchormen. The newsmen who anchor the major network newscasts are national figures, watched daily by many millions. In show business terms, they're the "stars" of broadcast journalism. As such, they are provided with everything it takes to put on the best possible newscast day after day, to build the ratings necessary to stay on top and, not too incidentally, to attract the national advertising that helps offset the enormous expenses in this kind of international news coverage.

By the time the network newscaster is ready to go before the cameras, he probably has spent a full work day preparing for that broadcast. Time is allotted for him to "read in," to familiarize himself with the day's run of news and to consult with the production and writing staffs. It is likely the newscaster has contributed in some degree to writing the script. If he has any question about anything, he can make use of the research staff maintained by the networks. In all probability, he has a trained researcher assigned to his own production to devote full time to digging out whatever tidbits of information are needed to enhance the editorial content. At least the final hour before broadcast ordinarily is spent going over, timing and marking the script, inserting last-second changes and coordinating details with the control room crew.

Beyond the editorial resources, the network anchorman has a host of individual experts to assist him. The networks assign experienced and talented makeup artists to each show, including the newscasts. Perhaps 15 minutes before each broadcast, a makeup man or woman arrives at the anchorman's office to apply the pancake makeup, the eye shadow or other cosmetics needed to make the anchor man appear and feel as comfortable as possible.

When the "star" steps onto the set, long hours and huge sums already have gone into the design and construction of that theater for news. With today's heavy reliance on such visual aids, most network newscasts use at least two and often three studio cameras. Before the broadcast, the newscaster must take a moment with the director to mark their scripts to make certain that they will be working with the same camera at the same time. Lighting experts who participated at the design stage make frequent checks to balance the studio lighting to make a pleasant picture for the audience and the best possible working situation for the performer. So exacting are the standards that, for instance, when network newscasts went to color, gray paper was introduced for script purposes to avoid any "bounce" or glare from the intense lighting needed on the set.

SCRIPT AND PROMPTER

One problem the network anchorman shares with his local counterpart is that of handling the script. With today's lengthening newscasts, the anchorman often is required to lug a great wad of paper before the camera and to manage it in such a way that it does not get in the way. Again, this is a matter of individual style and practice. When the anchorman sits at a desk, it is fairly common for him to place the script before him, to read a page and then move it as quietly as possible to the side when finished. In cases where an anchorman stands before the camera, he must learn to shuffle through page by page. Experienced speakers and performers usually develop their own techniques of reading in such a way as to minimize the feeling that a script is involved.

For the network performer, however, there is the assistance, if he wants it, of some kind of prompting device. When his script has been written and edited, a carbon copy

View from the rear of Studio 46, with John Hart on the CBS Morning News set. (Courtesy Norman Goldman)

Cameraman's view of Correspondent Hart through the studio camera viewfinder. (Courtesy Norman Goldman)

A prompting device as seen from the anchorman position.
(Courtesy Norman Goldman)

goes to a prompter team ordinarily made up of at least one typist and one technician. The typist converts the original typescript into large type selected for size by the anchorman. Prompter type ranges from five-eighth to three-quarter inch block letters and a copy is made for each studio camera. The script is typed on rolls of yellow paper, wound on reels and fixed directly over the lenses of the studio cameras. The prompter technician ordinarily is someone familiar with the production and the reading speed of the anchorman. He has a position on the studio floor and a control console with which he runs the prompting device, which is coordinated so that it runs in synchronization on all cameras. Thus, the anchorman has his script in hand for protection and at least occasional glances but, primarily, he is looking not into but just above the lens, to the prompting device that provides him with the facility of seeming to speak directly to those on the home side of the camera.

In the early days of television news, before the development of prompting systems, the script was a real problem. Veteran CBS News Correspondent, Douglas Edwards, tells many remarkable stories of some of the strange, wild and even ludicrous things that happened in the pioneer days. At one point, Edwards recalls, his producer, Don Hewitt, was so bugged by the script problem that he toyed with the idea of getting Edwards to learn to read Braille so that he could keep a Braille copy of the script under his desk and be able to read it right along, with only occasional glances down at the script before him on the desk. Happily for all concerned, the plan never was used!

PROBLEMS OF TIMING

Where the local newscaster must often devise his own method of receiving time cues, the network performer has a host of helpers keeping close check on the clock for him. Ultimate responsibility falls to the studio floor manager, who positions himself to the side of a camera. The floor manager gets his information via headphones from the control room, where time is checked to the second at least by an associate director and perhaps also by a production assistant and someone from the editorial staff. On cue from the director or the associate director, the floor manager relays messages mostly by hand signal to the newsman, telling him to speed his delivery, to slow it down, to cut his copy or to stretch it, or whatever is required to conform to time requirements. A

A moment to relax and look again at a filmed takeout on the air as the studio lights gleam down on John Hart. (Courtesy Norman Goldman)

network production must keep to time and much effort ordinarily is spent making sure it does.

The floor manager also assists the anchorman by pointing to the camera that will be used in the next shot, thereby helping to avoid the embarrassment of having the newsman face a camera that is not on the the air.

In addition to his contact through the floor manager, it is desirable for the anchorman to be linked directly to the control room through a tiny earphone over which the director can relay instructions even during periods when the anchorman actually is broadcasting. Minimal use of this system is desired, because of the danger of distracting the broadcaster, but it is still another safety device and channel for internal communication while a newscast is in progress. When the anchorman is not on camera, such as those times when film or tape is running or a live switch or commercial is in progress, it is possible for the performer to consult with the production or editorial staff on the studio telephone or to have someone go onto the studio floor to convey some information. This becomes necessary when major changes are made while the production is on the air. Perhaps a planned live switch has failed or a late film can be made ready for use on the newscast. Whatever the case, it is necessary to let the anchorman know what is happening, while the production crew gears itself for the change and the editorial staff writes whatever new copy is necessary to set up the new element. It might even be that the change simply is an editorial development requiring the substitution of copy during the course of the newscast. Up-dated copy can be handed to the anchorman when he is not on camera, hopefully at a point at which the broadcaster has enough time to look the item over.

SELF-PROTECTION

Television news is prepared and delivered by human beings, which means that occasional lapses, errors and other minor accidents do happen both on local and network productions. Since the advent of video tape, live switches on newscasts have become the exception rather than the rule they once were. Because of the constant danger of some kind of technical failure, it was standard practice on network newscasts to arm the anchorman with standby copy so that he could excuse the failure if it happened and give a brief summary of what the switch was to have contained. Today, it is much more common to take in a feed of news material and record it on video tape in advance of the newscast to reduce that possible failure. If the correspondent, who covered the story at some outlying place, goes to an affiliated station, or another station willing to provide the facilities for switching, and runs into any kind of difficulty during the advance feed, he can simply redo his material until he gets it right, providing, of course, that there was ample time to begin with. Today, it is commonplace for transcripts to be made of all switch or even filmed material in network productions. Then, the anchorman has a copy of those transcripts and can use them as standby copy, reading them entirely or in part in the event of a technical problem on the air. In those rare instances when live switches must be scheduled, it is wise to have someone check with the reporter making the feed so that standby copy can be written for the anchorman.

Even with the extensive chain of command in a network production, where professional writers, editors and producers, and the anchorman, himself, read—copy before it goes on air, time pressures and last-minute changes occasionally do contribute to letting factual errors go on the air. Then, too, the wire services also are capable of giving out misinformation that is not corrected until the newscast is in progress or over. Whatever the reason for the error, responsible newsmen are anxious to convey factually correct information. It can be an embarrassment for the anchorman, but when an error is caught on the air it is wiser to try to correct it as quickly as possible rather than to let it go. Obvious misstatements are likely to bring telephone calls from viewers who caught them. Less obvious errors will nag at the newsmen involved.

In quite a different category of the unpleasant things that can happen on the air are the ordinary "fluffs" that broadcasters, themselves, make. There are days when the tongue, the teeth, the lips and the hard palate just won't work together, and no matter how much preparation the newscaster has put into his effort, he will wind up slurring or mispronouncing words that ordinarily give him no trouble. If it happens once or twice in separate areas of a lengthy newscast, it is wiser just to go right on and not to call attention in any way to the minor difficulty. If he has the unhappy experience of one of those sudden, inexplicable flare-ups of fluffs, he might pause, laugh at himself if the material lends itself to a moment of levity, or otherwise pardon himself in a brief, gracious way. Basically, it is a matter of feeling one's way through an awkward situation.

Still another problem area, falling into the same play-it-by-ear category, is that of coughing or clearing the throat on the air. This is a situation in which the radio newscaster has the decided advantage over his television counterpart. The radio broadcaster usually has his own cutoff switch on the microphone he is using and can just flip the switch momentarily while he sneezes or clears his throat. The television newscaster has no place to go. He can just hope he won't run into the problem, and, again, excuse it away as graciously as possible if a sneeze happens or his voice fails him momentarily.

STUDIO ETIQUETTE

One final word of warning is in order when it comes to a broadcasting studio, radio or television. The smart thing for anyone in a studio—broadcaster, technician or visitor—is to watch what you say. In spite of all precautions, microphones sometimes are left open and the casual conversation that takes place when people aren't aware the studio is "hot" can find its way on the air. For the broadcaster, naturally, this is an ever more potent danger. Sometimes when things do go wrong, a broadcaster may forget himself at least momentarily and sound off about his displeasure. Far wiser it is for him to wait until after the production when he's out of the studio and the chance of his telling it all to his audience is nil.

CHAPTER 15

A Career in Broadcast Journalism

Year by year, the dimensions of broadcasting continue to broaden. The number of commercial and non-commercial television stations increases, as does the total of the AM and FM stations on the air. Educational television is a new and increasingly important force in broadcasting, and cable television is opening still another entire area. It is natural to expect, then, that the opportunities in broadcast journalism are expanding. Indeed, there is perhaps more room not just for expansion but also for more basic improvement than the surface statistics of radio and television would indicate.

The author examined a recent edition of the "Broadcasting Yearbook" and compiled figures on the practice of journalism within the television industry. The "Broadcasting Yearbook," as anyone familiar with it knows, lists each station and its key personnel, including the news director. While the way of doing things varies from station to station, it is safe to assume that a station listing a news director does have at least a one-man news staff and must pay at least some attention to local news. Conversely, it must be concluded that stations listing no news director are, in the case of network affiliates, just skinning by on the national and international news fed them by the network, and that independent stations listing no news director are doing as little as possible, or nothing at all, in providing news coverage of their viewing areas.

There appeared in this survey to be some correlation between network affiliation and news responsibility, because of the 515 affiliated stations checked, 434 listed news directors while 81 did not. Among independent stations, only 47 listed news directors while 80 did not. Some indication of the wide variations played on the journalistic theme can be found in the listing of one station which reports that its general manager serves also as sales manager and news director. Two others listed news directors who doubled as program directors. Only one station listed a female news director.

A check also was run on the educational stations on the air. One-hundred-and-sixty-one did not list a news director, while ten did. One of the ten was a combination general manager, program director and news director.

Allowing for a certain bias that places news in the essential category, the author was stunned to find that the management of so many commercial television stations can hold the viewers in such low regard as to minimize local news coverage. The lack of news coverage is much more easily understood in the case of educational stations, many of which must struggle just to stay on the air and do perform some kind of public service function by their very existence. Throughout this book there are references to what the author considers to be low quality performance in the news area, where newsmen are overworked and called upon to perform almost impossible tasks. It seems a safe enough assumption that stations which do not employ someone with the title of news director must be doing even less, perhaps having a staff announcer read an occasional news item if something happens in a community that the station simply cannot ignore.

It is to be hoped that the expansion of television will create competitive situations in which those stations that slough off this primary responsibility will be forced to change their method of operation.

CABLE TELEVISION

Throughout this book, the discussion has centered on commercial and educational television. As this volume was being completed, still another vast new area of television was beginning to open up. One thing that is apparent is that this new branch should hold many new opportunities for those who wish to broadcast.

This new arrival is Community Antenna Television (CATV) or cable television. CATV differs from conventional television only in that signals are sent over a cable rather than through the air. There are those who feel that by opening many new channels for entertainment and information, cable television can become the dominant communications medium in the United States. They speak in terms of a "wired nation" with an almost unlimited variety of program offerings.

Cable television actually has existed since 1949. Mostly, it has served as a booster medium, bringing clear television pictures from existing commercial and educational stations into areas where signals were weak. By 1952, there were 70 CATV systems in operation throughout the country, serving a mere 14,000 subscribers. The National Cable Television Association estimated that, as of March of 1970, there were

2,400 CATV systems serving 4,500,000 customers. The development of cable television has been slowed by its commercial competition and by governmental wrangling over how cable television should be regulated.

CATV had few problems at first, when it served only as an agent to improve reception of existing television programming. Then, when it began to move into areas where there was direct competition for advertising revenues, commercial interests went to the FCC for protection. The FCC responded by limiting the spread of cable television. The fine points of trying to work out an orderly expansion of cable television provide the bases for many proceedings still before the FCC, but 1971 was something of a breakthrough year for CATV operators.

Most new cable television systems are equipped to provide from 12 to 20 channels for programming. Because of federal restrictions and the expenses involved, most of that capacity remains unused. Many of the original small CATV operators are joining forces and moving into the area of program origination. The FCC spurred this development with a ruling that CATV systems with 3,500 or more subscribers must produce and originate program material of their own, on one of their channels (as of April 1, 1971). The obvious thrust of CATV is to provide local and special-interest programs, or what has been described as "grass roots" live programming. It is certain that as cable television grows in popularity and audience, it will create many new opportunities for newscasters and reporters.

GETTING THE FIRST JOB

The nation's colleges and universities are the "breeding grounds" of future journalists, and all aspirants are tortured by the worry of getting that first job. Journalism, generally, has provided an extreme example of that contradication where an employer wants to hire only young people with both education and experience. Young people aware of this ask themselves all the time how they can be expected to amass practical experience while preparing themselves academically. It is a dilemma, but too much time probably is spent in agonizing that could be better employed in an effort to make something happen.

Unquestionably, the easiest and quickest way to begin a career in broadcasting, or any other field, is to have the foresight to select parents, relatives or friends with either proprietary rights or good connections in the chosen area of effort. Most of us just aren't that fortunate, or wise! It was suggested earlier that young people can learn a lot about the practical side of broadcast journalism by making themselves acquainted with the personnel at local or nearby radio and television stations. An earnest, helpful individual should be able to make some friends that will draw on their own contacts within the field, especially if they think they detect some promise in the newcomer. For the energetic, there often are part-time jobs that provide experience and help with the enormous costs of education.

Since broadcasting has emerged as such a powerful and popular force in our national life, more and more educational institutions are moving to meet the demands of students for better and more advanced courses in the field. A survey made by the National Association of Broadcasters in 1970 showed that 223 colleges and universities then were offering courses in radio and television, as compared with only 147 two years earlier. Of the 223 4-year schools surveyed, 173 offered a Bachelor's degree course, 87 had a Master's curriculum, and 23 offered Doctorates. For the young men and women enrolled in a college course in communications, there often are opportunities to combine some experience with education by taking part in the broadcasting activities of the school's radio or television station. This cannot measure up to day-to-day experience, but it helps. Then, too, most colleges and universities provide some kind of placement service which should be able to give the job hunting senior some assistance.

Some of the 2-year colleges are also providing introductory courses to broadcasting, and broadcasting schools can be found in every major city in the United States. The educational opportunities, then, are plentiful. For those contemplating a career as a radio or television newscaster, however, there is an increasing need for deep and solid educational grounding to prepare the individual to understand the society in which he lives and works and the complex people who populate it.

More often than not, it will fall to the individual to break his own ground in the search for that first job and whether or not he has had help and guidance, he must make the decision on any employment opportunity. He must decide on the section of the country in which he wants to work, and then canvass the opportunities, make the contacts, arrange interviews, submit audition tapes and resumes, and generally follow the same practices that any other newcomer to any field of endeavor must pursue. Almost every state has an association of broadcasters that often serves as a clearing house of information on what stations need in the way of personnel. The "Broadcasting Yearbook" lists all professional organizations as well as every radio and television station either on the air or soon to begin broadcasting in the United States, Canada, Mexico and the Caribbean. The Yearbook gives the names of individuals for the job seeker to write to, along with addresses and telephone numbers. Still another source for job leads is "Broadcasting" magazine, which is published weekly and carries a section of help wanted ads.

It should be pointed out that a polite and interesting letter is the proper first step in approaching a potential employer. Many with jobs to offer are repelled by sloppy letters of application and resumes. A professional looking letter indicates that the applicant is both serious and industrious. It is insulting to send someone in a position of authority a poorly-duplicated letter or resume. Better practice is just to take the time to type letters individually and learn the name of someone to write to. A neatly drawn and cleanly duplicated resume usually is more acceptable when it goes along with a personalized covering letter. The central point here is that a young person often can make a fine initial impression with his first contact. He will be better off the more effort he puts into doing just that.

EXPANDING OPPORTUNITIES

While the broadening of a responsible approach to broadcast journalism should eventually produce wider opportunites for the individuals involved, already there are tremendous and improving opportunities for people with intelligence, talent and diligence. The newcomer just out of college might expect to serve an apprenticeship of a length that only he can determine in a small station. Careers are such individualized happenings, of course, that it is foolish to try to set any schedule or pattern. Some individuals with enormous personal drive must and will push on faster than others. There are those with eyes only for the pinnacle; a few will make it, but most will settle for less. Many sociologists say that future generations would be wise to prepare themselves not just for one lifetime career but instead for several different careers. Broadcasting is a medium, it would seem, that has that sort of flexibility built-in.

Someone who sets out on a career in broadcast journalism might fancy himself, or herself, as a performer and might find somewhere along the way that the inborn desire to "star" might better be satisfied on the stage. The kind of experience and training that broadcasting provides can only be helpful.

On the other hand, the aspiring "star" of the news field might find, as he or she climbs the ladder, that the increasing pressures of being out there in front of the microphone or the camera are too much for the sort of personality he or she has developed into. Such a personal discovery might well lead the individual to a career as a correspondent in which the desire to work in news, to report it and to broadcast at least occasionally can be combined. For the trained and experienced newsman or woman who suddenly discovers the need to abandon a position out front, there are opportunities in the production area in putting newscasts together or perhaps producing documentaries. The need for a basic writing skill has been stressed, and anyone with some talent and an editorial background usually can devise a way to make a living, either in newspaper, magazine or free-lance work.

For the person who finds himself or herself completely at home and satisfied in broadcast journalism, the opportunities are many. Perhaps from the small, independent station, the young person seeking a career might move up to a network affiliate in a good-sized city. After learning how that station wants things done, he can settle in for a while to practice and perfect his own repertorial and performing techniques. Many individuals can be content with the wages and notoriety that go with broadcasting for a station in this middle area. Often it is a relaxed, pleasant situation, with conscious attempts made to minimize the built-in pressures of the business. For those who need to try bigger things, opportunities exist to do at least occasional reports for the network. The alert newsman in any affiliate often can take advantage of situations in which he can discharge the responsibility to cover his own station on a news story or feature and then offer the network a companion report if the story does have national interest. Then, too, when network news officials get to know and like the work of someone at an affiliate, they often will call upon that person for coverage that can provide him with extra income and perhaps open the door to a network assignment if he desires one.

The person with an eye on the network must be ready to go where the network wants to send him and to become expert at the network method of covering news. For the aspiring network anchorman, it is a long and often difficult road. Networks generally follow the practice of training newcomers to network operations with a break-in period on the assignment desk, or whatever the network might call its central news-gathering unit. This assignment normally would bring the newcomer to network headquarters in New York City, where he ordinarily is given a few weeks to observe operations. Once he has the hang of it, he can expect to draw an assignment of indefinite duration on the overnight shift, which runs roughly from midnight to 8 AM. Ordinarily, that is the more or less quiet time, at least as far as domestic coverage is concerned. But, time differences overseas bring the overnight assignment editor well into the news day in Europe and the Pacific. He will keep close watch on the way the network's various arms function, actually will assign certain domestic coverage and arrange to get film from outside sources. When the new man has learned the network's ways, he might remain based in New York to cover news stories in the northeastern United States or else he might be sent to one of the network's news bureaus, for instance, in Chicago, Atlanta or Los Angeles. If he has a facility with a foreign language or a special knowledge of an overseas area, he might be put into one of the foreign bureaus, in London, Bonn, Moscow, Saigon or elsewhere.

Initially, the newcomer to the network will have the title of reporter. If he proves himself particularly good at covering the stories to which he is assigned, in writing high-quality reports and delivering them live, on film or on tape, he will be promoted eventually to correspondent. While individual stations often give the title of corespondent to anyone who reports for them, because it sounds professional, the networks are rather more jealous of the title and strive to make it mean true professionalism. In network operations, it is a mark of particular distinction and is won by individual talent and hard work. Correspondents, too, can either be assigned to work out of a particular bureau or based in New York or Washington, where the networks maintain large staffs.

As news expanded from the standard, 15-minute newscasts of the 1950s to the half-hour newscasts of the 1960s and into hour-long daily newscasts at the beginning of the 1970s, the networks have had to enlarge their news staffs and to carve out certain areas of expertise. It has long been traditional for the networks to have at least one correspondent assigned to the White House to cover all the varied activities of the president and to accompany him wherever he goes. More recently, it has become set practice to designate a congressional correspondent, a diplomatic correspondent, perhaps a Pentagon correspondent or a labor correspondent and set them loose to concentrate solely on their area of special interest. It is not uncommon for the networks to have a United Nations correspondent, a space correspondent and others who can be assigned at least temporarily to one particular area of human endeavor or government operation. These men report frequently, some almost daily, on their specialties and are well known not only within their field but also by the viewing public.

It is to the ranks of their correspondents that the networks ordinarily look when there is an anchor spot to fill. Millions of viewers get to know the correspondents, but a network anchorman is recognized by almost everyone who owns a television set. He is one of the "stars" of network television news and can command a salary running into six figures.

WAGES AND WORKING CONDITIONS

It is impossible to generalize about wage scales in broadcast journalism. At stations where newscasters are represented by AFTRA, there are contractually agreed minimums for base pay and commercial fees, which is to say that the broadcaster must be paid at least a specified amount for working a more or less normal week, plus so much extra for each commercially-sponsored newscast he reads on the air. Commercial sponsorship is vitally important to the income of a newscaster, since base pay ordinarily is set at average figures for the area and income expands with each additional commercial newscast the individual can handle. On the other hand, non-commercial or sustaining newscasts often mean the broadcaster can be called upon to do a lot of work and receive only the same base pay. Many newscasters find it wise to employ talent agents to negotiate contracts that go beyond the amounts specified by the AFTRA contract, in return for which the agent receives a percentage of the newscaster's earnings. Obviously, also, the newscaster must pay dues to his union. Here, again, it is the talent and industry a newscaster demonstrates that put him in the position of being able to demand high pay for his services.

At local stations where no union contract is involved, the newsman, of course, is on his own to negotiate whatever salary he can get. Obviously, when he feels his pay is unsatisfactory, the newsman must look elsewhere. Ordinarily, he will either visit or write to stations that interest him to make his availability known. Sometimes newsmen looking for work distribute demonstration audio or video tapes or films but they should always be prepared when looking for work to be asked to write and deliver an audition performance, which is a much more valid test of one's ability.

Working conditions vary from station to station and area to area. It is impossible to specify how much time should be spent in preparation for a newscast. Newscasters are human beings and some anchorman spend a full day getting set for one broadcast, while others less diligent will do as little as possible. The only safe generalization in this regard is that the top men in the business didn't get there by ease of effort and certainly don't stay there by applying their talent and energy sparingly.

The men who anchor the newscasts at stations around the country often become well-known within their viewing and listening areas and thus are at least minor celebrities. This, in turn, leaves them open for all manner of extra demands on their time from within and without the business. Professional and charitable organizations often ask them to address various functions or participate in some way in many worthwhile affairs. This, too, is part of the routine and must be handled skillfully by each individual in his own way.

When a newsman achieves the status of the top man at his station, or network, he will be called upon, also, for duties beyond his normal assignments. The anchormen at the major networks are usually the key men in the extended, special coverage given to political conventions and elections, space adventures and the other momentous events of our time. The same holds true at the local level. When a local station undertakes the not inconsiderable effort of putting on a special broadcast, it ordinarily would expect its number one man to be behind the microphone or in front of the camera. These extra assignments often involve long hours of "homework" to prepare for the event, along with rehearsals and taping sessions that must be squeezed in between normal chores. It still is a major facet of the news business, however, and, for the most part, the anchormen would be insulted if not called upon to make the extra effort.

Still another factor that should be taken into account by the young man or woman considering a career in broadcast journalism is that radio and television news is often a 24 hour-a-day, seven-day-a-week proposition. Irregular working hours are the rule in most branches of journalism, but especially in broadcasting. The people who broadcast the television news around the dinner hour usually work a day that brings them into the newsroom about ten or 11 o'clock in the morning and keeps them there until seven or eight PM. For the individuals who anchor the late news, usually at 11 PM, the work day might begin around two or three PM and last until all is quiet after the newscast, providing, of course, that there are no other duties to be performed that day.

Radio is particularly productive in the early hours of the day, when families are getting ready for work and school. For many broadcasters, then, it means arriving at news headquarters at hours that most working people simply don't believe. Someone responsible for writing and broadcasting a 15-minute newscast at eight AM would have to plan to be at his desk by five AM, and some work schedules are even more demanding than that.

Another peculiarity of the news business that outsiders can't understand is that, even though they want to see and hear their favorite newscasters on weekends and holidays, someone has to go to work to put those newscasts together and broadcast them on special days when it seems that everyone else is relaxing or enjoying family functions. Not only is it a problem to work on those occasions, but weekends and holidays often are slow news days when it becomes even more difficult to fill the allotted air time.

These are a few of the drawbacks of the business, but they hardly offset the excitement of working in a vital, important, fast-moving and every-changing field that offers rich rewards both in financial security and personal satisfaction for those who practice broadcast journalism with devotion and strive constantly for excellence.

Index

T

U

V